I0150603

Hindi Language:

101 Hindi Verbs

By Aditya Patel

Contents

Introduction to Hindi Verbs and Conjugations

Introduction to Hindi Verbs and Conjugations

In the vein of historical linguistics, Hindi is considered genetically related to English. Genetically relative implies that the languages were spoken by the same people who later separated. English is an Indo-European language that comes under the Germanic subfamily, whereas Hindi comes under the Romance subgroup of the same domain. Compared with English, Hindi has about half as many vowels and twice as many consonants. Compared with English, Hindi has weak, but predictable, word stress.

The structural and organizational differences in Hindi and English are mostly attributed to their word orders. Many members of a class of words function as the main elements of predicates that typically express action, state, or a relation between two things, and they may be inflected for tense, aspect, voice, mood, and to show agreement with subject or object (in modern descriptive linguistic analysis).

Verb is a word or group of words that functions as the sentence's predicate or introduces the predicate as modifier (a verb phrase). Verbs are doing words. A verb can express

- A physical action (for example, to swim, to write, to climb).
- A mental action (for example, to think, to guess, to consider).
- A state of being (for example, to be, to exist, to appear).

Verbs that express a state of being take a little practice to spot, but they are the most common.

A small, but important, group of verbs does not express any activity. The most important verb in this group—arguably, of all—is the verb *to be*. It is seen in forms such as *is, are, were, was, will be*, and so on.

Hindi verbs are inflected according to the gender of the subject (masculine, feminine), number of the subject (singular, plural), tense (present, past, future), action (perfect, imperfect, continuous), and degree of respect (intimate, familiar, respect).

Verbs are referred to in their Infinitive noun form, which ends in –na. Hindi verbs are words that convey action (bring, read, walk, run) or a state of being (exist, stand). In most languages, a verb may agree with the person, gender, and/or number of some of its arguments, such as its subject or object.

SUBJECT OF A VERB
The person or thing performing the verb's action is said to be the verb's subject or the sentence's subject.

DIRECT OBJECT OF A VERB
Many verbs perform an action on something. The "something" is called the verb's direct object.

1

INDIRECT OBJECT OF A VERB
Some verbs have two objects: a direct object (see above) and an indirect object. The indirect object is the person or thing for which the action was performed.

PASSIVE SENTENCE
A sentence's subject does not always do the verb's action. Sometimes, the action is done to the subject. Such sentences are called passive sentences because the subjects are passive, that is, not doing anything.

ACTIVE SENTENCE
Active sentences are opposite to passive sentences. In an active sentence, the verb's subject performs the action.

CONJUGATION OF VERBS
A verb changes its form a little depending on the subject. For example, the first three are the singular forms (first person singular, second person singular, and third person singular). The second three are the plural forms (first person plural, second person plural, and third person plural).

PARTICIPLES
Participles are formed from verbs. There are two types: present participles and past participles. Present participles end with -ing. Past participles have various endings.

Types of verbs
A *transitive verb* is a verb that has an object. An *intransitive verb* is a verb that does not have an object.

Transitive verbs need an object after them, and they take direct or indirect objects. When a verb has an object that receives the action of the verb, the verb is transitive.

Intransitive verbs do not need an object. They can be followed by a complement, usually an adjective or adverb. For example, the food smells good (subject + verb + complement). Intransitive verbs are action verbs, but unlike transitive verbs, they do not have an object receiving the action. An intransitive verb does not take a direct object. In other words, the action is not done to someone or something. It only involves the subject. For example:

वह **हँसा**—*Vah Hansa.* (He laughed.)
(*Laughed* is an intransitive verb. It has no direct object. You cannot laugh something.)

उसने एक चुटकुला **बताया था**—*Usne aik chutkula bataya tha.* (He told a joke.)

(*Told* is a transitive verb. The direct object is *a joke*. You can tell something. You can tell a story, a lie, a joke, and so on.)

Adverbs of frequency are words such as *often*, *sometimes*, and *never*.

Tenses of the verb

Tenses are necessary when learning Hindi. Tenses in Hindi help us understand what time an action occured. "I play," "I am playing," "I played," and "I will play" are examples of different tenses. The verb must be slightly modified (addition of -ing or -ed at the end) or supporting verbs must be used (use of "am" or "will") in order to express a verb in different tenses. These modifications to the verb must be made to express a verb in different tenses. We do this in English, and Hindi is the same. There are many examples to explain each tense:

- Present tense
- Present continuous tense
- Past tense
- Future tense

The below table summarizes the different tenses in Hindi.

Tenses in Hindi

1.	Present Indefinite Tense [See the table here for all pronouns.]	I read.	मैं **पढ़ता** हूँ l (main padhta hoon)
2.	Present Continuous Tense [See the table here for all pronouns.]	I am reading.	मैं **पढ़ रहा** हूँ l (main padh rahaa hoon)
3.	Present Perfect Tense	I have read.	मैंने **पढ़ा** है l (maine padhaa hai)
4.	Present Perfect Continuous Tense	I have been reading.	मैं **पढ़ता** रहा हूँ l (main padhtaa rahaa hoon)
1.	Past Indefinite Tense [See the table here for all pronouns.]	I read.	मैं **पढा** l (main padhaa)
2.	Past Continuous Tense	I was reading.	मैं **पढ़ रहा** था l (main padh rahaa thaa)

| 3. | Past Perfect Tense | I had read. | मैंने **पढा** था।(maine padhaa thaa) |
| 4. | Past Perfect Continous Tense | I had been reading. | मैं **पढ़ता रहा** था।main padhtaa rahaa thaa) |

1.	Future Indefinite Tense	I will read.	मैं **पढूंगा** ।(main padhunga)
2.	Future Continuous Tense.	I will be reading.	मैं **पढ़ता रहूंगा**।(main padhtaa rahunga)
3.	Future Perfect Tense	I will have read.	मैंने पढ़ लिया होगा।(maine padh liya hoga)
4.	Future Perfect Continuous Tense	I will have been reading.	मैं **पढ़ता रहा होउंगा**। (main padhataa rahaa houngaa)

The principle design of Hindi verbs is the synthesis of aspect and tense/mood.

Imperfective participle
The habitual aspect represents the imperfective participle and the perfective/perfect aspect represents the perfect participle. Tense and mood represent the various forms of होना. The present tense and indicative mood are represented by the present indicative forms of होना, the past tense and the indicative mood are represented by the past indicative forms of होना, the present tense and subjunctive mood are represented by the present subjunctive forms of होना,, and so on.

Imperfective participle + present subjunctive of होना = present habitual subjunctive.

Perfect participle + past tense of होना = past perfect indicative.

Perfect participle + present tense of होना = present perfect indicative.

And so on.

The indicative mood is the most common mood in Hindi and it is used to indicate statements regarding facts or ideas, and so on.

Present Habitual
The present habitual verb form combines the present tense with the habitual aspect, indicating habitual, frequent, or repeated actions in the present. It can also be used when making general statements. It has several idiomatic uses that are unrelated to the present tense or habitual aspect.

The present habitual form:
For example, the verb रहना, which means to stay,remain,live, orabide, रहता है is the third

person singular masculine present habitual formThe imperfective participle रहता) combines the

aspectual component with the temporal component (है). It could be translated as "he/she lives (someplace)."

वह दिल्ली में **रहती** है—*Vah Dilli me rehti hai.* ("She lives in Delhi.")

This is a factual statement.

मैं बहुत किताबें **पढ़ता** हूँ—*Main bahut kitaben padhta hun.* ("I read a lot of books.")

Uses of the Imperfective Participle + Present Tense Form of होना: Thereare several idiomatic uses that are not related to the present tense or habitual aspect of this verb form. The imperfective participle + present tense form of होना, when used in the third person plural may indicate an exhortation:

जाते हैं—*Jaate hain.* ("Let's go.")

खाते हैं—*Khaate hain.* ("Let's eat.")

The imperfective participle + present tense form of होना, which is frequently in the first person singular) indicates an action that is imminent:

आती हूँ—*Aati hun. (*"I'm coming."/"I'm just about to come."/"I'm coming right now."/) and so on.

निकलता हूँ—*Nikalta hun. (*"I'm going out/leaving."/"I'm just about to go out.")/ and so on.

Past Habitual
The past tense and habitual aspect are combined by the past habitual tense, The imperfective participle + past tense form of होना form the past habitual tense. It is usually translated in English as "used to . . ." as in "used to do," "used to eat," "used to go,"and so on.

Present Continuous
The present tense and the continuous aspect are combined by thepresent continuous verb form . The verb stem + perfect participle of रहना (रहा/रहे/रही) + present tense form of होना form the present continuous tense.

Past Continuous
The past tense and the continuous aspect are combined by the past continuous verb form. The verb stem + perfect participle of रहना (रहा/रहे/रही) + past tense form of होना form the past continuous tense.

Past Perfective
The past perfective is the same as the perfect participle. The perfective aspect and **past tense are combined by the past perfective tense.**

Present Perfect
The present perfect is a "perfect" verb form thatindicates the action is completed and has relevance in the present time. Perfect participle + present tense form of होना forms the present perfect tense.

Past Perfect
The past perfect is a "perfect" verb form that indicates the action is complete and was relevant at a past time. Perfect participle + past tense form of होना form the past perfect tense.

Future Tense
Verb stem + first suffix + second suffix form the future tense.The first set of suffixes are imperative. There are three different imperatives in Hindi: तू (tu), तुम (tum), and आप (aap) imperative. The tu imperative is the stem itself. The tum imperative is the stem + -o. The aap imperative is the stem + -ie or –iye.

Examples:
पानी **ला**—*Paani la.* ("Bring water.")(intimate)

पानी **लाओ**—*Paani lao.* ("Bring water.")(familiar)

पानी **लाइए**—*Paani laiye.* ("Bring water.")(respect)

The imperatives are made negative by adding मत (*mat*), ना (*na*), or नहीं (*nahin*). Use *mat* with the tu imperative. Use *mat* or *na* with the tum imperative. Use *na* or *nahin* with the aap imperative.

Examples:

वहाँ **मत** जा—*Vahan mat jaa.* ("Don't go there.")(intimate)

वहाँ **ना** जाओ—*Vahan na jao.* ("Don't go there.")(familiar)

वहाँ **नहीं जाइए**—*Vahan nahi jaiye.* ("Don't go there.")(respect)

To Have
There is no Hindi verb for "to have." Possession is expressed in other ways.

Movable Objects
Possession of movable objects is expressed using के पास (*ke pas*) after the (English) subject.

Examples:
राम **के पास** गाड़ी है—*Ram ke pas gaadi hai.* ("Ram has a car.")("Near Ram a car it is.")
मेरे **पास** किताब है—*Mere pas kitab hai.* ("I have a book.")("Near me a book it is.")

Immovable Objects
Possession of immovable objects and of relatives is expressed using the possessive particles *ka, ki, ke.*

Examples:
उस**का** मकान है—*Uska makaan hai.* ("He has a house.")("Of him a house it is.")
राम **के** दो बेटे हैं—*Ram ke do bete hai.* ("Ram has two sons.")("Of Ram two sons there are.")

Kriya (Verb in Hindi Grammar)
A. Kinds of Verbs
Sakarmak Kriya (Transitive verb)—These directly affect another person/object. These are of two types:

   1. *Preranarthak Kriya* (causative verb)
   2. *Dwikarmak Kriya* (verbs with two objects)

Akarmak Kriya (Intransitive verb)—These have no effect on others.

B. *Kaal* (Tense)

Bhoot Kaal (Past tense)—6 Types	*Vartman Kaal* (Present tense)—3 Types	*Bhavishya Kaal* (Future tense)—2 Types
1. *Samanya Bhoot*(Past indefinite) 2. *Aasann Bhoot* (Past imminent) 3. *Apurn Bhoot*(Past continuous) 4. *Purna Bhoot* (Past perfect) 5. *Sandigdh Bhoot* (Past doubtful) 6. *Hetuhetumad Bhoot* (Past conditional)	1. *Samanya Vartman* (Present indefinite) 2. *Apurn Vartman* (Present continuous) 3. *Sandigdh Vartman* (Present doubtful)	1. *Samanya Bhavishya* (Future indefinite) 2. *Sambhavya Bhavishya* (Future conditional or doubtful)

C. *Vachya* (Voice)

These are three types:

Kartri Vachya (Active voice)

Karm Vachya (Passive voice)

Bhav Vachya (Impersonal voice)

Therefore, words that represent an action or state of being, such as *go*, *strike*, *travel*, and *exist* are examples of verbs. A verb is the essential part of the predicate of a sentence. The grammatical forms of verbs include number, person, and tense.

Infinitive	To Accept	स्वीकार करना *Sweekar karna*

Indicative

Present	Past
स्वीकार करता हूँ - I accept *Sweekar karta hun*	स्वीकार करता **था** - I accepted *Sweekar karta tha*

Preterite And Perfect	Pluperfect
स्वीकार किया **हुआ** - It is accepted *Sweekar kiya hua*	स्वीकार किया **था** - I had accepted *Sweekar kiya tha*

Future And Immediate Future	Immediate Past Future
स्वीकार करूँगा - I will accept *Sweekar karunga*	स्वीकार करने वाला **था** - I was about to accept *Sweekar krne wala tha*

Imperative

Single And Polite	Future Polite
स्वीकार **कीजिये** - Do accept Sweekar **kijiye**	स्वीकार कीजिए**गा** - Please accept Sweekar kijie**ga**

Subjunctive

Present	Habitual And Continuous
स्वीकार **करूँ** - Do I accept Sweekar **karun**	स्वीकार करता **हूँ** - I accept Sweekar karta **hun**

Perfect And Immediate Future
स्वीकार किया है - I have accepted Sweekar kara **hun**

Conditional

Present And Habitual	Continuous And Preterite
स्वीकार **करता** है- He accepts *Sweekar **karta hai***	स्वीकार कर रहा **होता** - He would be accepting *Sweekar **kar** raha **hota***

Presumptive

Present And Imperfective	Continuous And Future Perfect
स्वीकार करता **हूँगा** – I would be accepting. *Sweekar karta **hunga***	स्वीकार कर रहा **हूँगा**- I would have been accepting. *Sweekar **kar** raha **hunga***

Infinitive	To dance	नृत्य करना Nritya karna

Indicative

Present	Past
नृत्य करता हूँ - I dance Nritya karta **hun**	नृत्य करता **था** - I danced Nritya karta **tha**

Preterite And Perfect	Pluperfect
नृत्य किया **हुआ** - It is danced Nritya kiya **hua**	नृत्य किया **था** - I had danced Nritya kiya **tha**

Future And Immediate Future	Immediate Past Future
नृत्य करूँगा - I will dance Nritya karun**ga**a	नृत्य करने वाला **था** - I was about to dance Nritya karne vala **tha**

Imperative

Single And Polite	Future Polite
नृत्य करिए - dance Nritya **kariye**	नृत्य कीजिए**गा** - Please dance Nritya kijie**ga**

Subjunctive

Present	Habitual And Continuous
नृत्य **करूँ** – Do I dance Nritya **karoon**	नृत्य करता रहा **हूँ** - I dance Nritya karta raha **hun**

Perfect And Immediate Future
नृत्य किया है - I have danced Nritya kiya hai

Conditional	

Present And Habitual	Continuous And Preterite
नृत्य **करता** है- He dances Nritya **karta hai**	नृत्य कर रहा **होता** - He would be dancing Nritya **kar** raha **hota**

Presumptive	

Present And Imperfective	Continuous And Future Perfect
नृत्य करता **हूँगा** – I would be dancing. Nritya karta **hunga**	नृत्य कर रहा **हूँगा**- I would have been dancing. Nritya **kar** raha **hunga**

Infinitive	To Decide	निश्चय करना Nishchay karna

Indicative

Present	Past
निश्चय करता हूँ - I decide Nishchay karta **hun**	निश्चय किया **था** - I decided Nishchay kiya **tha**

Preterite And Perfect	Pluperfect
निश्चय किया **हुआ** - It is decided Nishchay kiya **hua**	निश्चय किया **था** - I had decided Nishchay kiya **tha**

Future And Immediate Future	Immediate Past Future
निश्चय करूँगा - I will decide Nishchay karun**ga**	निश्चय करने वाला **था** - I was about to decide Nishchay karne vala **tha**

Imperative	

Single And Polite	Future Polite
निश्चय **करिए** - Do decide Nishchay **kariye**	निश्चय कीजिए**गा** - Please decide Nishchay kijie**ga**

Subjunctive	

Present	Habitual And Continuous
निश्चय **करूँ** - Do I decide Nishchay **karoon**	निश्चय करता रहा **हूँ** - I decide Nishchay karta **hun**

Perfect And Immediate Future
निश्चय कर लिया है - I have decided Nishchay kar liya hai

Conditional

Present And Habitual	Continuous And Preterite
निश्चय **करता** है- He decides Nishchay **karta hai**	निश्चय कर रहा **होता** - He would be deciding Nishchay **kar** raha **hota**

Presumptive

Present And Imperfective	Continuous And Future Perfect
निश्चय करता **हूँगा** – I would be deciding. Nishchay karta **hunga**	निश्चय कर रहा **हूँगा**- I would have been deciding. Nishchay **kar** raha **hunga**

Infinitive	To Decrease	कम करना Kam karna

Indicative

Present	Past
कम करता हूँ - I decrease Kam karta **hun**	कम करता **था** - I decreased Kam karta **tha**

Preterite And Perfect	Pluperfect
कम किया **हुआ** - It is decreased Kam kiya **hua**	कम किया **था** - I had decreased Kam kiya **tha**

Future And Immediate Future	Immediate Past Future
कम करूँगा - I will decrease Kam karun**ga**a	कम करने वाला **था** - I was about to decrease Kam karne vala **tha**

Imperative

Single And Polite	Future Polite
कम **करिए** - Do decrease Kam **kariye**	कम कीजिए**गा** - Please decrease Kam kijie**ga**

Subjunctive

Present	Habitual And Continuous
कम **करूँ** - Do I decrease Kam **karoon**	कम करता **हूँ** - I decrease Kam karta **hun**

Perfect And Immediate Future
कम किया है - I have decreased Kam kiya है**n**

Conditional

Present And Habitual	Continuous And Preterite
कम **करता** - He decreases Kam **karta**	कम कर रहा **होता** - He would be decreasing Kam **kar** raha **hota**

Presumptive

Present And Imperfective	Continuous And Future Perfect
कम करता **हूँगा** – I would be decreasing. Kam karta **hunga**	कम कर रहा **हूँगा**- I would have been decreasing. Kam **kar** raha **hunga**

Infinitive	To Die	मरना marna

Indicative

Present	Past
मरता **हूँ** - I die Marta **hun**	मरता **था** - I died Marta **tha**

Preterite And Perfect	Pluperfect
मरा **हुआ** - It is dead	मरा **था** - I had died

Future And Immediate Future	Immediate Past Future
मरूँगा - I will die Marun**ga**	मरने वाला **था** - I was about to die Marne vala **tha**

Imperative

Single And Polite	Future Polite
मरा **करिए** - Do die	मरिए**गा** - Please die
Maraa **kariye**	marie**gaa**

Subjunctive

Present	Habitual And Continuous
मरा **करूँ** - Do I die	मरता **हूँ** - I die
Mara **hun**	Marta **hun**

Perfect And Immediate Future
मर गया **हूँ** - I have died
Mara gaya **hun**

Conditional

Present And Habitual	Continuous And Preterite
मरता - He dies Marta	मर रहा **होता** - He would be dying Mara raha **hota**

Presumptive

Present And Imperfective	Continuous And Future Perfect
मरता **हूँगा** – I would be dying. Marta **hunga**	मर रहा **हूँगा**- I would have been dying. Mar raha **hunga**

Infinitive	To Do	कार्य करना Karya karna

Indicative

Present	Past
कार्य करता हूँ - I do Karya karta **hun**	कार्य करता **था** - I did Karya karta **tha**

Preterite And Perfect	Pluperfect
कार्य किया **हुआ** है- It is done Karya kiya **hua hai**	कार्य किया **था** - I had done Karya kiya **tha**

Future And Immediate Future	Immediate Past Future
कार्य कर**ूँगा** - I will do Karya karun**ga**	कार्य करने वाला **था** - I was about to do Karya karne vala **tha**

Imperative

Single And Polite	Future Polite
कार्य **करिए** - Do Karya **kariye**	कार्य कीजिएगा - Please do Karya kijie**ga**

Subjunctive

Present	Habitual And Continuous
कार्य **करूँ** - Do I do Karya karuun	कार्य करता हूँ - I do Karya karta **hun**

Perfect And Immediate Future
कार्य कर लिया है- I have done Karya kara liya hai

Conditional

Present And Habitual	Continuous And Preterite
कार्य **करता** है- He does Karya karta hai	कार्य कर रहा **होता** - He would be doing Karya **kar** raha **hota**

Presumptive

Present And Imperfective	Continuous And Future Perfect
कार्य करता **हूँगा** – I would be doing. Karya karta **hunga**	कार्य कर रहा **हूँगा**- I would have been doing. Karya **kar** raha **hunga**

Infinitive	To Drink	पीना peena

Indicative

Present	Past
पीता हूँ - I drink Peeta **hun**	पीता **था** - I drank Peeta **tha**

Preterite And Perfect	Pluperfect
पिया **हुआ** - It is drunk Piya **hua**	पिया **था** - I had drunk Piya **tha**

Future And Immediate Future	Immediate Past Future
पिऊँगा - I will drink Piunga	पीने वाला **था** - I was about to drink Peene vala **tha**

Imperative

Single And Polite	Future Polite
पीजिए - Do drink Peejiye	पीजिएगा - Please drink Peejie**ga**a

Subjunctive

Present	Habitual And Continuous
पियू - Do I drink Peeyu	पीता रहा - I drink Peta **hun**

Perfect And Immediate Future
पिया हूँ - I have drunk Piya **hun**

Conditional

Present And Habitual	Continuous And Preterite
पीता - He drinks Peeta	पी रहा **होता** - He would be drinking Pee raha **hota**

Presumptive

Present And Imperfective	Continuous And Future Perfect
पीता **हूँगा** – I would be drinking. Peeta **hunga**	पी रहा **हूँगा**- I would have been drinking. Pee raha **hunga**

Infinitive	To Drive	वाहन चलाना Vahan chalana

Indicative

Present	Past
वाहन चलाता **हूँ** - I drive Vahan chalata **hun**	वाहन चलाता **था** - I drove Vahan chalata **tha**

Preterite And Perfect	Pluperfect
वाहन चलाया **हुआ** - It is driven Vahan chalaya **hua**	वाहन चलाया **था** - I had driven Vahan chalaya **tha**

Future And Immediate Future	Immediate Past Future
वाहन चलाउन्गा - I will drive Vahan chalaun**gaa**	वाहन चलाने वाला **था** - I was about to drive Vahan chalane vala **tha**

Imperative

Single And Polite	Future Polite
वाहन चलाईए - Do drive Vahan chalaiye	वाहन चलाईए**गा** - Please drive Vahan chalaie**ga**

Subjunctive

Present	Habitual And Continuous
वाहन चलाऊँ- Do I drive Vahan chalaun	वाहन चलाता रहा हूँ - I drive Vahan chalata रहा **hun**

Perfect And Immediate Future
वाहन चलाया है - I have driven Vahan chalaya hai

Conditional

Present And Habitual	Continuous And Preterite
वाहन चलाता - He drives Vahan chalata	वाहन चला रहा **होता** - He would be driving Vahan chala raha ho**ga**

Presumptive

Present And Imperfective	Continuous And Future Perfect
वाहन चलाता **हूँगा** – I would be driving. Vahan chalata **hunga**	वाहन चला रहा **हूँगा**- I would have **been** driving. Vahan chala raha **hunga**

Infinitive	To Eat	खाना khana

Indicative

Present	Past
खाता हूँ - I eat Khata **hun**	खाता **था** - I ate Khata **tha**

Preterite And Perfect	Pluperfect
खाया **हुआ** - It is eaten Khaya **hua**	खाया **था** - I had eaten Khay **tha**

Future And Immediate Future	Immediate Past Future
खाउंगा - I will eat khaun**ga**	खाने वाला **था** - I was about to eat Khane vala **tha**

Imperative

Single And Polite	Future Polite
खाईए - Do eat Khaeeye	खाएगा - Please eat Khaega

Subjunctive

Present	Habitual And Continuous
खाना खाऊँ - Do I eat Khana khaoon	खाता रहा हूँ - I eat Khata raha hun

Perfect And Immediate Future
खाया हूँ - I have eaten   Khaya hun

Conditional

Present And Habitual	Continuous And Preterite
खाता - He eats Khata	खा रहा **होता** - He would be eating Kha raha **hota**

Presumptive

Present And Imperfective	Continuous And Future Perfect
खाता **हूँगा** – I would be eating. Khata **hunga**	खा रहा **हूँगा**- I would have been eating. Kha raha **hunga**

Infinitive	To Enter	प्रवेश करना Pravesh karna

Indicative

Present	Past
प्रवेश करता हूँ - I enter Pravesh karta **hun**	प्रवेश करता **था** - I entered Pravesh karta **tha**

Preterite And Perfect	Pluperfect
प्रवेश किया **हुआ** - It is entered Pravesh kiyu **hua**	प्रवेश किया **था** - I had entered Pravesh kiya **tha**

Future And Immediate Future	Immediate Past Future
प्रवेश करूँगा - I will enter Pravesh karun**ga**	प्रवेश करने वाला **था** - I was about to enter Pravesh karne vala **tha**

Imperative

Single And Polite	Future Polite
प्रवेश **करिए** - Do enter Pravesh **kariye**	प्रवेश **कीजिएगा** - Please enter Pravesh kijie**ga**

Subjunctive

Present	Habitual And Continuous
प्रवेश **करूँ** - Do I enter Pravesh **karun**	प्रवेश करता हूँ - I enter Pravesh karta **hun**

Perfect And Immediate Future
प्रवेश कर गया हूँ - I have entered Pravesh kara gaya **hun**

Conditional

Present And Habitual	Continuous And Preterite
प्रवेश **करता** - He enters Pravesh karta	प्रवेश कर रहा **होता** - He would be entering Pravesh **kar** raha **hota**

Presumptive

Present And Imperfective	Continuous And Future Perfect
प्रवेश करता **हूँगा** – I would be entering. Pravesh karta **hunga**	प्रवेश कर रहा **हूँगा**- I would have been entering. Pravesh **kar** raha **hunga**

Infinitive	To Exit	निकास करना Nikaas karna

Indicative

Present	Past
निकास करता हूँ – I exit Nikaas karta **hun**	निकास करता **था** – I exited Nikaas karta **tha**

Preterite And Perfect	Pluperfect
निकास किया **हुआ** – It is exited Nikaas kiya **hua**	निकास किया **था** – I had exited Nikaas kiya **tha**

Future And Immediate Future	Immediate Past Future
निकास करूँगा – I will exit Nikaas karun**ga**	निकास करने वाला **था** – I was about to exit Nikaas karne vala **tha**

Imperative

Single And Polite	Future Polite
निकास **करिएर** - Do exit Nikaas **kariye**	निकास कीजिए**गा** - Please exit Nikaas kijie**ga**

Subjunctive

Present	Habitual And Continuous
निकास **करूँ** – Do I exit Nikaas **karun**	निकास करता हूँ – I exit Nikaas karta **hun**

Perfect And Immediate Future
निकास कर गया हूँ - I have exited Nikaas kara gaya **hun**

Conditional

Present And Habitual	Continuous And Preterite
निकास **करता** - He exits Nikaas karta	निकास कर रहा **होता** - He would be exiting Nikaas **kar** raha **hota**

Presumptive

Present And Imperfective	Continuous And Future Perfect
निकास करता **हूँगा** – I would be exiting. Nikaas karta **hunga**	निकास कर रहा **हूँगा** - I would have been exiting. Nikaas **kar** raha **hunga**

Infinitive	To Explain	वर्णन करना Varnan karna

Indicative

Present	Past
वर्णन करता हूँ - I explain Varnan karta **hun**	वर्णन करता **था** - I explained Varnan karta **tha**

Preterite And Perfect	Pluperfect
वर्णन किया **हुआ** - It is explained Varnan kiya **hua**	वर्णन किया **था** - I had explained Varnan kiya **tha**

Future And Immediate Future	Immediate Past Future
वर्णन करूँगा - I will explain Varnan karun**ga**	वर्णन करने वाला **था** - I was about to explain Varnan karne vala **tha**

Imperative

Single And Polite	Future Polite
वर्णन **करिए** - Do explain Varnan **kariye**	वर्णन कीजिए**गा** - Please explain Varnan kijie**ga**

Subjunctive

Present	Habitual And Continuous
वर्णन **करूँ** - Do I explain Varnan **karun**	वर्णन करता हूँ - I explain Varnan karta **hun**

Perfect And Immediate Future
वर्णन कर दिया है - I have explained Varnan kar diya hai**n**

Conditional

Present And Habitual	Continuous And Preterite
वर्णन **करता** है- He explains Varnan karta है	वर्णन कर रहा **होता** - He would be explaining Varnan **kar** raha **hota**

Presumptive

Present And Imperfective	Continuous And Future Perfect
वर्णन करता **हूँगा** – I would be explaining. Varnan karta **hunga**	वर्णन कर रहा **हूँगा**- I would have been explaining. Varnan **kar** raha **hunga**

Infinitive	To Fall	गिरना Girna

Indicative

Present	Past
गिरता हूँ - I fall Girta **hun**	गिरता **था** - I fell Girta **tha**

Preterite And Perfect	Pluperfect
गिरा **हुआ** - It is fallen Gira **hua**	गिरा **था** - I had fallen Gira **tha**

Future And Immediate Future	Immediate Past Future
गिरूँगा - I will fall Girun**ga**	गिरने वाला **था** - I was about to fall Girne vala **tha**

Imperative

Single And Polite	Future Polite
गिरिएर - Do fall Giriye	गिरिएगा – Please fall Giriega

Subjunctive

Present	Habitual And Continuous
गिरूँ – Do I fall girun	गिरता हूँ – I fall Girta hun

Perfect And Immediate Future
गिरा हूँ - I have fallen Gira hun

Conditional

Present And Habitual	Continuous And Preterite
गिरता - He falls Girta	गिर रहा **होता** - He would be falling Gir raha **hota**

Presumptive

Present And Imperfective	Continuous And Future Perfect
गिरता **हूँगा** – I would be falling. Girta **hunga**	गिर रहा **हूँगा**- I would have been falling. Gir raha **hunga**

Infinitive	To Feel	अनुभव करना Anubhav karna

Indicative

Present	Past
अनुभव करता हूँ - I feel Anubhav karta **hu**	अनुभव करता **था** - I felt Anubhav karta **tha**

Preterite And Perfect	Pluperfect
अनुभव किया **हुआ** - It is felt Anubhav kiya **hua**	अनुभव किया **था** - I had felt Anubhav kiya **tha**

Future And Immediate Future	Immediate Past Future
अनुभव करूँगा - I will feel Anubhav karun**ga**	अनुभव करने वाला **था** - I was about to feel Anubhav karne vala **tha**

Imperative

Single And Polite	Future Polite
अनुभव **करिए** - Do feel Anubhav **kariye**	अनुभव कीजिए**गा** - Please feel Anubhav kijie**ga**

Subjunctive

Present	Habitual And Continuous
अनुभव **करूँ** – Do I feel Anubhav karun	अनुभव करता हूँ - I feel Anubhav karta **hun**

Perfect And Immediate Future
अनुभव किया है - I have felt Anubhav kiya hai**n**

Conditional

Present And Habitual	Continuous And Preterite
अनुभव **करता** है- He feels Anubhav karta hai	अनुभव कर रहा **होता** - He would be feeling Anubhav **kar** raha **hota**

Presumptive

Present And Imperfective	Continuous And Future Perfect
अनुभव करता **हूँगा** – I would be feeling. Anubhav karta **hunga**	अनुभव कर रहा **हूँगा**- I would have been feeling. Anubhav **kar** raha **hunga**

Infinitive	To Fight	लड़ाई करना Ladaai karna

Indicative

Present	Past
लड़ाई करता हूँ - I fight Ladaai karta **hun**	लड़ाई करता **था** - I fought Ladaai karta **tha**

Preterite And Perfect	Pluperfect
लड़ाई की हुई - It is fought Ladaai kee hui	लड़ाई की थी - I had fought Ladaai kee thee

Future And Immediate Future	Immediate Past Future
लड़ाई करूँगा - I will fight Ladaai karun**ga**	लड़ाई करने वाला **था** - I was about to fight Ladaai karne vala **tha**

Imperative

Single And Polite	Future Polite
लड़ाई **करिए** - Do fight Ladaai **kariye**	लड़ाई कीजिए**गा** - Please fight Ladaai kijie**ga**

Subjunctive

Present	Habitual And Continuous
लड़ाई **करूँ** - Do I fight Ladaai **karun**	लड़ाई करता **हूँ** - I fight Ladaai karta **hun**

Perfect And Immediate Future
लड़ाई करा **हूँ** - I have fought Ladaai kara **hun**

Conditional

Present And Habitual	Continuous And Preterite
लड़ाई **करता** है - He fights Ladaai karta hai	लड़ाई कर रहा **होता** - He would be fighting Ladaai **kar** raha **hota**

Presumptive

Present And Imperfective	Continuous And Future Perfect
लड़ाई करता **हूँगा** – I would be fighting. Ladaai karta **hunga**	लड़ाई कर रहा **हूँगा**- I would have been fighting. Ladaai **kar** raha **hunga**

Infinitive	To Find	खोज करना Khoj karna

Indicative

Present	Past
खोज करता हूँ - I find Khoj karta **hun**	खोज करता **था** - I found Khoj karta **tha**

Preterite And Perfect	Pluperfect
खोज किया **हुआ** - It is found Khoj kiya **hua**	खोजा **था** - I had found Khoja **tha**

Future And Immediate Future	Immediate Past Future
खोज करूँगा - I will find Khoj karun**ga**	खोज करने वाला **था** - I was about to find Khoj karne vala **tha**

Imperative	

Single And Polite	Future Polite
खोज **करिए** - Do find Khoj **kariye**	खोज कीजिए**गा** - Please find Khoj kijie**ga**

Subjunctive	

Present	Habitual And Continuous
खोज **करूँ** - Do I find Khoj **karun**	खोज करता **हूँ** - I find Khoj karta **hun**

Perfect And Immediate Future
खोज कर ली है - I have found Khoj kara lee hai

Conditional

Present And Habitual	Continuous And Preterite
खोज **करता** है - He finds Khoj karta hai	खोज कर रहा **होता** - He would be finding Khoj **kar** raha **hota**

Presumptive

Present And Imperfective	Continuous And Future Perfect
खोज करता **हूँगा** – I would be finding. Khoj karta **hunga**	खोज कर रहा **हूँगा**- I would have been finding. Khoj **kar** raha **hunga**

Infinitive	To Finish	समाप्त करना Samapt karna

Indicative

Present	Past
समाप्त करता हूँ - I finish Samapt karta **hun**	समाप्त करता **था** - I finished Samapt karta **tha**

Preterite And Perfect	Pluperfect
समाप्त किया **हुआ** - It is finished Samapt kiya **hua**	समाप्त किया **था** - I had finished Samapt kiya **tha**

Future And Immediate Future	Immediate Past Future
समाप्त करूँगा - I will finish Samapt karun**ga**	समाप्त करने वाला **था** - I was about to finish Samapt karne vala **tha**

Imperative

Single And Polite	Future Polite
समाप्त **करिए** - Do finish Samapt **kariye**	समाप्त कीजिए**गा** - Please finish Samapt kijie**ga**

Subjunctive

Present	Habitual And Continuous
समाप्त **करूँ** - Do I finish Samapt **karu**	समाप्त करता **हूँ** - I finish Samapt karta **hu**

Perfect And Immediate Future
समाप्त करा **हूँ** - I have finished Samapt kara **hu**

Conditional

Present And Habitual	Continuous And Preterite
समाप्त **करता** है- He finishes Samapt karta hai	समाप्त कर रहा **होता** - He would be finishing Samapt **kar** raha **hota**

Presumptive

Present And Imperfective	Continuous And Future Perfect
समाप्त करता **हूँगा** – I would be finishing. Samapt karta **hunga**	समाप्त कर रहा **हूँगा**- I would have been finishing. Samapt **kar** raha **hunga**

Infinitive	To Fly	उड़ना Udna

Indicative

Present	Past
उड़ता हूँ - I fly Udta **hun**	उड़ता **था** - I flied Udta **tha**

Preterite And Perfect	Pluperfect
उड़ा **हुआ** - It is flowned Udaa **hua**	उड़ा **था** - I had flied Udaa **tha**

Future And Immediate Future	Immediate Past Future
उड़ूँगा - I will fly Udun**ga**	उड़ने वाला **था** - I was about to fly Udne vala **tha**

Imperative

Single And Polite	Future Polite
उड़िए - Do fly Udiye	उड़िएगा - Please fly udiegaa

Subjunctive

Present	Habitual And Continuous
उड़ा करूँ - Do I fly Udaa karun	उड़ता हूँ - I fly Udta hun

Perfect And Immediate Future
उड़ा हूँ - I have flownflied Uda hun

Conditional

Present And Habitual	Continuous And Preterite
उड़ा **करता** है - He flies Udaa karta hai	उड़ रहा **होता** - He would be flying Udd raha **hota**

Presumptive

Present And Imperfective	Continuous And Future Perfect
उड़ता **हूँगा** – I would be flying. Udta **hunga**	उड़ रहा **हूँगा**- I would have been flying. Udd raha **hunga**

Infinitive	To forget	विस्मृत करना Vismrit karna

Indicative

Present	Past
विस्मृत करता **हूँ** – I forget Vismrit karta **hu**	विस्मृत करता **था** – I forgetted Vismrit karta **tha**

Preterite And Perfect	Pluperfect
विस्मृत किया **हुआ** – It is forgetted Vismrit kiya **hua**	विस्मृत किया **था** – I had forgetted Vismrit kiya **tha**

Future And Immediate Future	Immediate Past Future
विस्मृत करूँ**गा** – I will forget Vismrit karun**ga**	विस्मृत करने वाला **था** – I was about to forget Vismrit karne vala **tha**

Imperative

Single And Polite	Future Polite
विस्मृत **करिए** - Do forget Vismrit **kariye**	विस्मृत कीजिए**गा** - Please forget Vismrit kijie**ga**

Subjunctive

Present	Habitual And Continuous
विस्मृत कर**ूँ** - Do I forget Vismrit **karun**	विस्मृत करता **हूँ** - I forget Vismrit karta **hun**

Perfect And Immediate Future
विस्मृत करा **हूँ** - I have forgotten Vismrit kara **hun**

Conditional

Present And Habitual	Continuous And Preterite
विस्मृत **करता** है - He forgets Vismrit karta hai	विस्मृत कर रहा **होता** - He would be forgetting Vismrit **kar** raha **hota**

Presumptive

Present And Imperfective	Continuous And Future Perfect
विस्मृत करता **हूँगा** – I would be forgetting. Vismrit karta **hunga**	विस्मृत कर रहा **हूँगा** - I would have been forgetting. Vismrit **kar** raha **hunga**

Infinitive	To Get up	उठना Uthna

Indicative

Present	Past
उठा हूँ - I get up Utha hun	उठा **था** - I got up Utha tha

Preterite And Perfect	Pluperfect
उठा **हुआ** - It is up Utha hua	उठा **था** - I had got up Utha tha

Future And Immediate Future	Immediate Past Future
उठूँगा - I will get up Uthunga	उठने वाला **था** - I was about to get up Uthna vala **tha**

Imperative

Single And Polite	Future Polite
उठिए - Do get up Uthiye	उठिएगा - Please get up uthiegaa

Subjunctive

Present	Habitual And Continuous
उठा करूँ - Do I get up Utha karun	उठा हूँ - I get up Utha hun

Perfect And Immediate Future
उठा गया हूँ - I have got up Uth gaya hun

Conditional

Present And Habitual	Continuous And Preterite
उठता है - He gets up Utha **hai**	उठ रहा **होता** - He would be getting up Uth raha **hota**

Presumptive

Present And Imperfective	Continuous And Future Perfect
उठा **हूँगा** – I would be getting up Utha **hunga**	उठ रहा **हूँगा**- I would have been getting up Uth raha **hunga**

Infinitive	To Give	दान करना Daan karna

Indicative

Present	Past
दान करता **हूँ** - I give Daan karta **hun**	दान करता **था** - I gave Daan karta **tha**

Preterite And Perfect	Pluperfect
दान किया **हुआ** - It is given Daan kiya **hua**	दान किया **था** - I had given Daan kiya **tha**

Future And Immediate Future	Immediate Past Future
दान करूँगा - I will give Daan karun**ga**	दान करने वाला **था** - I was about to give Daan karne vala **tha**

Imperative

Single And Polite	Future Polite
दान **करिए** - Do give Daan **kariye**	दान कीजिए**गा** - Please give Daan kijie**ga**

Subjunctive

Present	Habitual And Continuous
दान **करूँ** - Do I give Daan **karun**	दान करता **हूँ** - I give Daan karta **hun**

Perfect And Immediate Future
दान किया है - I have given Daan किया है

Conditional

Present And Habitual	Continuous And Preterite
दान **करता** है- He gives Daan karta है	दान कर रहा **होता** - He would be giving Daan **kar** raha **hota**

Presumptive

Present And Imperfective	Continuous And Future Perfect
दान करता **हूँगा** – I would be giving. Daan karta **hunga**	दान कर रहा **हूँगा**- I would have been giving. Daan **kar** raha **hunga**

Infinitive	To Go	चला जाना Chala jana

Indicative

Present	Past
चला जाता हूँ - I go Chala jata **hun**	चला जाता **था** - I went Chala jata **tha**

Preterite And Perfect	Pluperfect
चला गया - It is gone Chala **ga**ya	चला गया **था** - I had gone Chala **gaya tha**

Future And Immediate Future	Immediate Past Future
चला जाउन्गा - I will go Chala jaun**ga**	चला जाने वाला **था** - I was about to go Chala jane vala **tha**

Imperative

Single And Polite	Future Polite
चले जाईए - Do go Chale jaaiye	चले जाईएगा - Please go Chale jaiega

Subjunctive

Present	Habitual And Continuous
चला करूँ - Do I go Chala karun	चला जाता हूँ - I go Chala jata hun

Perfect And Immediate Future
चला गया हूँ - I have gone Chala gaya hun

Conditional

Present And Habitual	Continuous And Preterite
चला जाता - He goes Chala jata	चला जा रहा **होता** - He would be going Chala jaa raha **hota**

Presumptive

Present And Imperfective	Continuous And Future Perfect
चला जाता **हूँगा** – I would be going. Chala jata **hunga**	चला जा रहा **हूँगा**- I would have been going. Chala jaa raha **hunga**

Infinitive	To Happen	हो जाना Ho jana

Indicative

Present	Past
हो जाता हूँ - I happen Ho jata **hun**	हो जाता **था** - I happened Ho jata **tha**

Preterite And Perfect	Pluperfect
हो गया - It is happened Ho **gaya**	हो गया **था** - I had happened Ho **gaya tha**

Future And Immediate Future	Immediate Past Future
होगा - I will happen ho**ga**	हो जाने वाला **था** - I was about to happen Ho jaane vala **tha**

Imperative

Single And Polite	Future Polite
हो जाईए - Do happen Ho jaiye	होईएगा - Please happen Hoiega

Subjunctive

Present	Habitual And Continuous
हुआ करूँ - Do I happen **Hua karun**	हो जाता हूँ - I happen Ho jata **hun**

Perfect And Immediate Future
हुआ हूँ - I have happened **Hua hun**

Conditional

Present And Habitual	Continuous And Preterite
हो जाता है- He happens Ho jata hai	हो रहा **होता** - He would be happening Ho raha **hota**

Presumptive

Present And Imperfective	Continuous And Future Perfect
होता हूँगा – I would be happening. **Hota hu**nga	हो रहा **हूँगा**- I would have been happening. Ho raha **hu**nga

Infinitive	To Have	होना Hona

Indicative

Present	Past
होता हूँ - I have **Hota hun**	**होता था** - I had **Hota tha**

Preterite And Perfect	Pluperfect
हुआ - It had **Hua**	हो गया **था** - I had Ho **gaya** **tha**

Future And Immediate Future	Immediate Past Future
हो**गा** - I will have Ho**ga**	होने वाला **था** - I was about to have Hone vala **tha**

Imperative	

Single And Polite	Future Polite
हो - Do have Ho	होएगा - Please have Hoe**ga**

Subjunctive	

Present	Habitual And Continuous
हुआ करूँ - Do I have **Hua karun**	होता हूँ - I have **Hota hun**

Perfect And Immediate Future
हुआ हूँ - I have had **Hua hun**

Conditional	

Present And Habitual	Continuous And Preterite
होता - He has Hota	हो रहा होता - He would be having Ho raha hota

Presumptive	

Present And Imperfective	Continuous And Future Perfect
होता हूँगा – I would be having. Hota hunga	हो रहा हूँगा- I would have been having. Ho raha hunga

Infinitive	To Hear	सुनना Sunna

Indicative

Present	Past
सुनता हूँ - I hear Suntan **hun**	सुनता **था** - I heard Sunta **tha**

Preterite And Perfect	Pluperfect
सुना **हुआ** - It is heard Suna **hua**	सुना **था** - I had heard Suna **tha**

Future And Immediate Future	Immediate Past Future
सुनूँगा - I will hear sunun**ga**	सुनने वाला **था** - I was about to hear Sunne vala **tha**

Imperative

Single And Polite	Future Polite
सुना **करिए** - Do hear Suna **kariye**	सुनिए**गा** - Please hear Sunie**ga**

Subjunctive

Present	Habitual And Continuous
सुना **करूँ** - Do I hear Suna **karun**	सुना करता **हूँ** - I hear Suna karta **hun**

Perfect And Immediate Future
सुना **है** - I have heard Suna **hai**

Conditional

Present And Habitual	Continuous And Preterite
सुनता है - He hears Sunta hai	सुना **होता** - He would be hearing Suna **hota**

Presumptive

Present And Imperfective	Continuous And Future Perfect
सुनता **हूँगा** – I would be hearing. Suntan **hunga**	सुन रहा **हूँगा**- I would have been hearing. Sun raha **hunga**

Infinitive	To Help	मदद करना Madad karna

Indicative

Present	Past
मदद करता हूँ - I help Madad karta **hun**	मदद करता **था** - I helped Madad karta **tha**

Preterite And Perfect	Pluperfect
मदद किया **हुआ** - It is helped Madad kiya **hua**	मदद किया **था** - I had helped Madad kiya **tha**

Future And Immediate Future	Immediate Past Future
मदद करूँगा - I will help Madad karun**ga**	मदद करने वाला **था** - I was about to help Madad karne vala **tha**

Imperative

Single And Polite	Future Polite
मदद **करिए** - Do help Madad **kariye**	मदद कीजिए**गा** - Please help Madad kijie**ga**

Subjunctive

Present	Habitual And Continuous
मदद **करूँ** - Do I help Madad **karun**	मदद करता **हूँ** - I help Madad karta **hun**

Perfect And Immediate Future
मदद की है- I have helped Madad kee hai

Conditional

Present And Habitual	Continuous And Preterite
मदद **करता** है- He helps Madad karta hai	मदद कर रहा **होता** - He would be helping Madad **kar** raha **hota**

Presumptive

Present And Imperfective	Continuous And Future Perfect
मदद करता **हूँगा** – I would be helping. Madad karta **hunga**	मदद कर रहा **हूँगा**- I would have been helping. Madad **kar** raha **hunga**

Infinitive	To Hold	पकड़ना pakadna

Indicative

Present	Past
पकड़ता हूँ - I hold Pakadta **hun**	पकड़ता **था** - I held Pakadta **tha**

Preterite And Perfect	Pluperfect
पकड़ा **हुआ** - It is held Pakada **hua**	पकड़ा **था** - I had held Pakada **tha**

Future And Immediate Future	Immediate Past Future
पकडूँगा - I will hold pakadun**ga**	पकड़ने वाला **था** - I was about to hold Pakadne vala **tha**

Imperative

Single And Polite	Future Polite
पकड़िए - Do hold Pakadiye	पकड़िएगा - Please hold Pakadiega

Subjunctive

Present	Habitual And Continuous
पकड़ूँ - Do I hold Pakadun	पकड़ता हूँ - I hold Pakadta hun

Perfect And Immediate Future
पकड़ा हूँ - I have held Pakda hun

Conditional

Present And Habitual	Continuous And Preterite
पकड़ता - He holds Pakadta	पकड़ रहा **होता** - He would be holding Pakad raha **hota**

Presumptive

Present And Imperfective	Continuous And Future Perfect
पकड़ता **हूँगा** – I would be holding. Pakadta **hunga**	पकड़ रहा **हूँगा**- I would have been holding. Pakad raha **hunga**

Infinitive	To Increase	आरोह करना Aaroh karna

Indicative

Present	Past
आरोह करता **हूँ** - I increase Aaroh karta **hun**	आरोह करता **था** - I increased Aaroh karta **tha**

Preterite And Perfect	Pluperfect
आरोह किया **हुआ** - It is increased Aaroh kiya **hua**	आरोह किया **था** - I had increased Aaroh kiya **tha**

Future And Immediate Future	Immediate Past Future
आरोह करूँगा - I will increase Aaroh karun**ga**	आरोह करने वाला **था** - I was about to increase Aaroh karne vala **tha**

Imperative

Single And Polite	Future Polite
आरोह **करिए** - Do increase Aaroh **kariye**	आरोह कीजिए**गा** - Please increase Aaroh kijie**ga**

Subjunctive

Present	Habitual And Continuous
आरोह **करूँ** - Do I increase Aaroh **karun**	आरोह करता **हूँ** - I increase Aaroh karta **hu**

Perfect And Immediate Future
आरोह किया है - I have increased Aaroh kiya hai**n**

Conditional

Present And Habitual	Continuous And Preterite
आरोह **करता** - He increases Aaroh karta	आरोह कर रहा **होता** - He would be increasing Aaroh **kar** raha **hota**

Presumptive

Present And Imperfective	Continuous And Future Perfect
आरोह करता **हूँगा** – I would be increasing. Aaroh karta **hunga**	आरोह कर रहा **हूँगा**- I would have been increasing. Aaroh **kar** raha **hunga**

Infinitive	To Introduce	परिचय करना Parichay karna

Indicative

Present	Past
परिचय करता **हूँ** - I introduce Parichay karta **hun**	परिचय करता **था** - I introduced Parichay karta **tha**

Preterite And Perfect	Pluperfect
परिचय किया **हुआ** - It is introduced Parichay kiya **hua**	परिचय किया **था** - I had introduced Parichay kiya **tha**

Future And Immediate Future	Immediate Past Future
परिचय कर**ूँगा** - I will introduce Parichay karun**ga**	परिचय करने वाला **था** - I was about to introduce Parichay karne vala **tha**

Imperative

Single And Polite	Future Polite
परिचय **करिए** - Do introduce Parichay **kariye**	परिचय कीजिए**गा** - Please introduce Parichay kijie**ga**

Subjunctive

Present	Habitual And Continuous
परिचय **करूँ** - Do I introduce Parichay **karun**	परिचय करता हूँ - I introduce Parichay karta **hun**

Perfect And Immediate Future
परिचय किया है - I have introduced Parichay kiya hai

Conditional

Present And Habitual	Continuous And Preterite
परिचय **करता** - He introduces Parichay karta	परिचय कर रहा **होता** - He would be introducing Parichay **kar** raha **hota**

Presumptive

Present And Imperfective	Continuous And Future Perfect
परिचय करता **हूँगा** – I would be introducing. Parichay karta **hunga**	परिचय कर रहा **हूँगा**- I would have been introducing. Parichay **kar** rah **hunga**

Infinitive	To Invite	आमंत्रित करना Aamantrit karna

Indicative

Present	Past
आमंत्रित करता **हूँ** - I invite Aamantrit karta **hun**	आमंत्रित करता **था** - I invited Aamantrit karta **tha**

Preterite And Perfect	Pluperfect
आमंत्रित किया **हुआ** - It is invited Aamantrit kiya **hua**	आमंत्रित किया **था** - I had invited Aamantrit kiya **tha**

Future And Immediate Future	Immediate Past Future
आमंत्रित करूँ**गा** - I will invite Aamantrit karun**ga**	आमंत्रित करने वाला **था** - I was about to invite Aamantrit karne vala **tha**

Imperative

Single And Polite	Future Polite
आमंत्रित **करिए** - Do invite Aamantrit **kariye**	आमंत्रित कीजिए**गा** - Please invite Aamantrit kijie**ga**

Subjunctive

Present	Habitual And Continuous
आमंत्रित **करूँ** - Do I invite Aamantrit **karun**	आमंत्रित करता **हूँ** - I invite Aamantrit karta **hun**

Perfect And Immediate Future
आमंत्रित करा **हूँ** - I have invited Aamantrit kara **hun**

Conditional

Present And Habitual	Continuous And Preterite
आमंत्रित **करता** - He invites Aamantrit karta	आमंत्रित कर रहा **होता** - He would be inviting Aamantrit **kar** raha **hota**

Presumptive

Present And Imperfective	Continuous And Future Perfect
आमंत्रित करता **हूँगा** – I would be inviting. Aamantrit karta **hunga**	आमंत्रित कर रहा **हूँगा**- I would have been inviting. Aamantrit **kar** raha **hunga**

Infinitive	To Kill	मारना
		Maarna

Indicative

Present	Past
मारता हूँ - I kill	मारता **था** - I killed
Maarta **hun**	Maarta **tha**

Preterite And Perfect	Pluperfect
मारा **हुआ** - It is killed	मारा **था** - I had killed
Maara **hua**	Maara **tha**

Future And Immediate Future	Immediate Past Future
मारूँगा - I will kill	मारने वाला **था** - I was about to kill
Maaru**nga**	Maarne vala **tha**

Imperative	

Single And Polite	Future Polite
मारा **करिए** - Do kill Maara **kariye**	मारिए**गा** - Please kill Maarie**ga**

Subjunctive	

Present	Habitual And Continuous
मारा **करूँ** – Do I kill Maara **karun**	मारता **हूँ** – I kill Maarta **hun**

Perfect And Immediate Future
मारा **हूँ** – I have killed Maara **hun**

Conditional	

Present And Habitual	Continuous And Preterite
मारता - He kills Maarta	मार रहा **होता** - He would be killing Maar raha **hota**

Presumptive	

Present And Imperfective	Continuous And Future Perfect
मारता **हूँगा** – I would be killing. Maarta **hunga**	मार रहा **हूँगा**- I would have been killing. Maar raha **hunga**

Infinitive	To Kiss	चुंबन करना Chumban karna

Indicative

Present	Past
चुंबन करता हूँ - I kiss Chumban karta **hun**	चुंबन करता **था** - I kissed Chumban karta **tha**

Preterite And Perfect	Pluperfect
चुंबन किया **हुआ** - It is kissed Chumban kiya **hua**	चुंबन किया **था** - I had kissed Chumban kiya **tha**

Future And Immediate Future	Immediate Past Future
चुंबन करूँगा - I will kiss Chumban karun**ga**	चुंबन करने वाला **था** - I was about to kiss Chumban karne vala **tha**

Imperative

Single And Polite	Future Polite
चुंबन **करिए** - Do kiss Chumban **kariye**	चुंबन कीजिए**गा** - Please kiss Chumban kijie**ga**

Subjunctive

Present	Habitual And Continuous
चुंबन **करूँ** - Do I kiss Chumban **karun**	चुंबन करता हूँ - I kiss Chumban karta **hun**

Perfect And Immediate Future
चुंबन किया है - I have kissed Chumban kara **hun**

Conditional

Present And Habitual	Continuous And Preterite
चुंबन **करता** - He kisses Chumban karta	चुंबन कर रहा **होता** - He would be kissing Chumban **kar** raha **hota**

Presumptive

Present And Imperfective	Continuous And Future Perfect
चुंबन करता **हूँगा** – I would be kissing. Chumban karta **hunga**	चुंबन कर रहा **हूँगा**- I would have been kissing. Chumban **kar** raha **hunga**

Infinitive	To Know	जानना Jaanna

Indicative

Present	Past
जानता हूँ - I know Jaanta **hun**	जानता **था** - I know Jaanta **tha**

Preterite And Perfect	Pluperfect
जाना **हुआ** - It is known Jaana **hua**	जाना **था** - I had knownJaana **tha**

Future And Immediate Future	Immediate Past Future
जानूँगा - I will know Jaanoonga	जानने वाला **था** - I was about to know Jaanne vala **tha**

Imperative

Single And Polite	Future Polite
जानिए - Do know Jaan**iye**	जानिएगा - Please know Jaanii**ega**

Subjunctive

Present	Habitual And Continuous
जानूँ - Do I know Jaanoon	जानता जाताहूँ - I know Jaanta jaata **hun**

Perfect And Immediate Future
जान रहाहूँ - I have known Jaan raha **hun**

Conditional

Present And Habitual	Continuous And Preterite
जानता - He knows Jaanta	जान रहा **होता** - He would be knowing Jaanraha **hota**

Presumptive

Present And Imperfective	Continuous And Future Perfect
जानता **हूँगा** – I would be knowing. Jaanta **hunga**	जान रहा **हूँगा**- I would have been knowing. Jaan raha **hunga**

Infinitive	To Laugh	हँसना Hansna

Indicative

Present	Past
हँसता **हूँ** - I laugh Hansta **hun**	हँसता **था** - I laughed Hansta **tha**

Preterite And Perfect	Pluperfect
हँसा - It is laughed Hansa **hua**	हँसा - I had laughed Hansa **tha**

Future And Immediate Future	Immediate Past Future
हँसाकरूँगा - I will laugh Hansa karun**ga**	हँसने वाला **था** - I was about to laugh Hansne vala **tha**

Imperative

Single And Polite	Future Polite
हँसा **करिए** - Do laugh Hansa **kariye**	हँसएगा - Please laugh hanse**ga**

Subjunctive

Present	Habitual And Continuous
हँसा **करूँ** - Do I laugh Hansa **karun**	हँसता हूँ - I laugh Hansta **hun**

Perfect And Immediate Future
हँसा हूँ - I have laughed Hansa **hun**

Conditional

Present And Habitual	Continuous And Preterite
हँसता - He laughs hansta	हँस रहा **होता** - He would be laughing Hans raha **hota**

Presumptive

Present And Imperfective	Continuous And Future Perfect
हँसता **हूँगा** – I would be laughing. Hansta **hunga**	हँस रहा **हूँगा**- I would have been laughing. Hans raha **hunga**

Infinitive	To Learn	याद करना Yaad karna

Indicative

Present	Past
याद करता हूँ - I learn Yaad karta **hun**	याद करता **था** - I learned Yaad karta **tha**

Preterite And Perfect	Pluperfect
याद किया **हुआ** - It is learned Yaad kiya **tha**	याद किया **था** - I had learned Yaad kiya **tha**

Future And Immediate Future	Immediate Past Future
याद करूँगा - I will learn Yaad karun**ga**	याद करने वाला **था** - I was about to learn Yaad karne vala **tha**

Imperative

Single And Polite	Future Polite
याद **करिए** - Do learn Yaad **kariye**	याद कीजिए**गा** - Please learn Yaad kijie**ga**

Subjunctive

Present	Habitual And Continuous
याद **करूँ** - Do I learn Yaad **karun**	याद करता **हूँ** - I learn Yaad karta **hun**

Perfect And Immediate Future
याद किया है - I have learned Yaad kiya hai **hun**

Conditional

Present And Habitual	Continuous And Preterite
याद **करता** - He learns Yaad karta	याद कर रहा **होता** - He would be learning Yaad **kar** rah **hota**

Presumptive

Present And Imperfective	Continuous And Future Perfect
याद करता **हूँगा** – I would be learning. Yaad karta **hunga**	याद कर रहा **हूँगा**- I would have been learning. Yaad **kar** raha **hunga**

Infinitive	To Lie down	लेट जाना Let jana

Indicative

Present	Past
लेटता हूँ - I lie down Letata **hun**	लेटता **था** - I lied down Letata **tha**

Preterite And Perfect	Pluperfect
लेटा **हुआ** - It is lied down Leta **hua**	लेटा **था** - I had lied down Leta **tha**

Future And Immediate Future	Immediate Past Future
लेटूँगा - I will lie down Letun**ga**	लेटने वाला **था** - I was about to lie down Letne vala **tha**

Imperative

Single And Polite	Future Polite
लेट जाईए - Do lie down Let jaiye	लेट जाईएगा - Please lie down Let jaiega

Subjunctive

Present	Habitual And Continuous
लेटा करूँ - Do I lie down Leta karun	लेट जाता हूँ - I lie down Let jata hun

Perfect And Immediate Future
लेटा हूँ - I have lied down Leta hun

Conditional

Present And Habitual	Continuous And Preterite
लेटता - He lies down Letata	लेट रहा **होता** - He would be lying down Let raha **hota**

Presumptive

Present And Imperfective	Continuous And Future Perfect
लेटता **हूँगा** – I would be lying down Letata **hunga**	लेट जा रहा **हूँगा**- I would have been lying down. Let jaa raha **hunga**

Infinitive	To Like	पसंद करना Pasand karna

Indicative

Present	Past
पसंद करता हूँ - I like Pasand karta **hun**	पसंद करता **था** - I liked Pasand karta **tha**

Preterite And Perfect	Pluperfect
पसंद किया **हुआ** - It is liked Pasand kiya **hua**	पसंद किया **था** - I had liked Pasand kiya **tha**

Future And Immediate Future	Immediate Past Future
पसंद करूँ**गा** - I will like Pasand karun**ga**	पसंद करने वाला **था** - I was about to like Pasand karne vala **tha**

Imperative

Single And Polite	Future Polite
पसंद **करिए** - Do like Pasand **kariye**	पसंद **कीजिएगा** - Please like Pasand kijie**ga**

Subjunctive

Present	Habitual And Continuous
पसंद **करूँ** - Do I like Pasand **karun**	पसंद करता **हूँ** - I like Pasand karta **hun**

Perfect And Immediate Future
पसंद किया है - I have liked Pasand kiya hai

Conditional

Present And Habitual	Continuous And Preterite
पसंद **करता** - He likes Pasand karta	पसंद कर रहा **होता** - He would be liking Pasand **kar** rahaa **hota**

Presumptive

Present And Imperfective	Continuous And Future Perfect
पसंद करता **हूँगा** – I would be liking. Pasand karta **hunga**	पसंद कर रहा **हूँगा**- I would have been liking. Pasand **kar** raha **hunga**

Infinitive	To Listen	सुनना sunna

Indicative

Present	Past
सुनता हूँ - I listen Sunta **hun**	सुनता **था** - I listened Sunta **tha**

Preterite And Perfect	Pluperfect
सुना **हुआ** - It is listened Suna **hua**	सुना **था** - I had listened Suna **tha**

Future And Immediate Future	Immediate Past Future
सुनूँगा - I will listen sunun**ga**	सुनने वाला **था** - I was about to listen Sunne vala **tha**

Imperative

Single And Polite	Future Polite
सुना करिए - Do listen Suna **kariye**	सुनिएगा - Please listen Suine**ga**

Subjunctive

Present	Habitual And Continuous
सुना करूँ - Do I listen Suna **karun**	सुनता हूँ - I listen Suntan **hun**

Perfect And Immediate Future
सुना हूँ - I have listened Suna **hun**

Conditional	

Present And Habitual	Continuous And Preterite
सुना **करता** - He listens Suna karta	सुन रहा **होता** - He would be listening Sun raha **hota**

Presumptive	

Present And Imperfective	Continuous And Future Perfect
सुनता **हूँगा** – I would be listening. Suntan **hunga**	सुन रहा **हूँगा**- I would have been listening. Sun rah **hunga**

Infinitive	To Live	निवास करना Niwaas karna

Indicative

Present	Past
निवास करता हूँ - I live Niwaas karta **hun**	निवास करता **था** - I lived Niwaas karta **tha**

Preterite And Perfect	Pluperfect
निवास किया **है** - It is lived Niwaas kiya **hai**	निवास किया **था** - I had lived Niwaas kiya **tha**

Future And Immediate Future	Immediate Past Future
निवास करूँ**गा** - I will live Niwaas karun**ga**	निवास करने वाला **था** - I was about to live Niwaas karne vala **tha**

Imperative

Single And Polite	Future Polite
निवास **करिए** - Do live Niwaas **kariye**	निवास कीजिए**गा** - Please live Niwaas kijie**ga**

Subjunctive

Present	Habitual And Continuous
निवास **करूँ** – Do I live Niwaas **karun**	निवास करता **हूँ** - I live Niwaas karta **hun**

Perfect And Immediate Future
निवास करा **हूँ** - I have lived Niwaas kara **hun**

Conditional

Present And Habitual	Continuous And Preterite
निवास **करता** - He lives Niwaas karta	निवास कर रहा **होता** - He would be living Niwaas **kar** raha **hota**

Presumptive

Present And Imperfective	Continuous And Future Perfect
निवास करता **हूँगा** – I would be living. Niwaas karta **hunga**	निवास कर रहा **हूँगा**- I would have been living. Niwaas **kar** raha **hunga**

Infinitive	To Lose	खोना Khona

Indicative

Present	Past
खोता हूँ - I lose Khota hun	खोता था - I lost Khota tha

Preterite And Perfect	Pluperfect
खो गया - It is lost Kho gaya	खो गया था - I had lost Kho gaya tha

Future And Immediate Future	Immediate Past Future
खोया करूँगा - I will lose Khoya karunga	खोने वाला था - I was about to lose Khone vala tha

Imperative

Single And Polite	Future Polite
खोईए - Do lose Khoeeye	खोईएगा - Please lose Khoie**ga**

Subjunctive

Present	Habitual And Continuous
खोया **करूँ** - Do I lose Khoya **karun**	खोता **हूँ** - I lose K**hota hun**

Perfect And Immediate Future
खो दिया है - I have lost Kho diya hai

Conditional

Present And Habitual	Continuous And Preterite
खोता - He loses khota	खो रहा **होता** - He would be losing Kho raha **hota**

Presumptive

Present And Imperfective	Continuous And Future Perfect
खोता **हूँगा** – I would be losing. Khota hunga	खो रहा **हूँगा**- I would have been losing. Kho raha **hunga**

Infinitive	To Love	प्रेम करना Prem karna

Indicative

Present	Past
प्रेम करता **हूँ** - I love Prem karta **hun**	प्रेम करता **था** - I loved Prem karta **tha**

Preterite And Perfect	Pluperfect
प्रेम किया **हुआ** - It is loved Prem kiya hua	प्रेम किया **था** - I had loved Prem kiya tha

Future And Immediate Future	Immediate Past Future
प्रेम क**रूँगा** - I will love Prem karun**ga**	प्रेम करने वाला **था** - I was about to love Prem karne vala **tha**

Imperative

Single And Polite	Future Polite
प्रेम **करिए** - Do love Prem **kariye**	प्रेम कीजिए**गा** - Please love Prem kijie**ga**

Subjunctive

Present	Habitual And Continuous
प्रेम **करूँ** - Do I love Prem **karun**	प्रेम करता **हूँ** - I love Prem karta **hun**

Perfect And Immediate Future
प्रेम किया है - I have loved Prem kiya hai**hun**

Conditional

Present And Habitual	Continuous And Preterite
प्रेम **करता** - He loves Prem karta	प्रेम कर रहा **होता** - He would be loving Prem **kar** raha **hota**

Presumptive

Present And Imperfective	Continuous And Future Perfect
प्रेम करता **हूँगा** – I would be loving. Prem karta **hunga**	प्रेम कर रहा **हूँगा**- I would have been loving. Prem **kar** raha **hunga**

Infinitive	To sit down	बैठना *baithna*

Indicative

Present	Past
बैठता हूँ - I sit down *Baithta* **hun**	बैठता **था** - I sat down *Baithta* **tha**

Preterite And Perfect	Pluperfect
बैठा **हुआ** - It is sat down *Baitha hua*	बैठा **था** - I had sat down *Baitha tha*

Future And Immediate Future	Immediate Past Future
बैठा करूँगा - I will sit down *Baitha karunga*	बैठने वाला **था** - I was about to sit down *Baithne vala* **tha**

Imperative

Single And Polite	Future Polite
बैठिए - Do sit down *Baithiye*	बैठिएगा - Please sit down *Baitiega*

Subjunctive

Present	Habitual And Continuous
बैठूँ - Do I sit down *Baithun*	बैठता हूँ - I sit down *Baithta hun*

Perfect And Immediate Future
बैठा हूँ - I have sat down *Baitha hun*

Conditional

Present And Habitual	Continuous And Preterite
बैठता - He sits down *Baithta*	बैठ रहा **होता** - He would be sitting down *Baith raha **hota***

Presumptive

Present And Imperfective	Continuous And Future Perfect
बैठता **हूँगा** – I would be sitting down. *Baithta **hunga***	बैठ रहा **हूँगा**- I would have been sitting down. *Baith raha **hunga***

Infinitive	To Sleep	सोना *Sona*

Indicative

Present	Past
सोता हूँ - I sleep *Sota hun*	सोता **था** - I slept *Sota tha*

Preterite And Perfect	Pluperfect
सोया **हुआ** - It is slept *Soya hua*	सोया **था** - I had slept *Soya tha*

Future And Immediate Future	Immediate Past Future
सोया कर**ूँगा** - I will sleep *Soya karunga*	सोने वाला **था** - I was about to sleep *Sone vala tha*

Imperative

Single And Polite	Future Polite
सोईए - Do sleep *Soeeye*	सोईएगा - Please sleep *Soiega*

Subjunctive

Present	Habitual And Continuous
सोऊँ - Do I sleep *Soun*	सोता रहता हूँ - I sleep *Sota rahta hun*

Perfect And Immediate Future
सोया हूँ - I have slept *Soya hun*

Conditional	

Present And Habitual	Continuous And Preterite
सोता - He sleeps Sota	सो रहा **होता** - He would be sleeping So raha **hota**

Presumptive	

Present And Imperfective	Continuous And Future Perfect
सोता **हूँगा** – I would be sleeping. Sota **hunga**	सो रहा **हूँगा**- I would have been sleeping. So raha **hunga**

Infinitive	To Smile	मुस्कुराना *Muskurana*

Indicative

Present	Past
मुस्कुराता **हूँ** - I smile *Muskurata* **hun**	मुस्कुराता **था** - I smiled *Muskurata* **tha**

Preterite And Perfect	Pluperfect
मुस्कुराना **हुआ** - It is smiled *Muskura* **hua**	मुस्कुराया **था** - I had smiled *Muskuraya* **tha**

Future And Immediate Future	Immediate Past Future
मुस्कुराना करूँगा - I will smile *Muskura karun***ga**	मुस्कुराने वाला **था** - I was about to smile *Muskurane vala* **tha**

Imperative

Single And Polite	Future Polite
मुस्कुराईए - Do smile *Muskuraeeye*	मुस्कुराईए**गा** - Please smile *Muskuraie**ga***

Subjunctive

Present	Habitual And Continuous
मुस्कुराता हूँ - Do I smile *Muskura hoon karun*	मुस्कुराता रहता हूँ - I smile *Muskurata rahta **hun***

Perfect And Immediate Future
मुस्कुराया हूँ - I have smiled *Muskuraya **hun***

Conditional

Present And Habitual	Continuous And Preterite
मुस्कुराता - He smiles *Muskurata*	मुस्कुरा रहा **होता** - He would be smiling *Musku raha **hota***

Presumptive

Present And Imperfective	Continuous And Future Perfect
मुस्कुराता **हूँगा** – I would be smiling. *Muskurata **hunga***	मुस्कुरा रहा **हूँगा**- I would have been smiling. *Muskura raha **hunga***

Infinitive	To Speak	वचन बोलना *Vachan bolna*

Indicative

Present	Past
वचन बोलता हूँ - I speak *Vachan bolta* **hun**	वचन बोलता **था** - I spoke *Vachan bolta* **tha**

Preterite And Perfect	Pluperfect
वचन बोला **हुआ** - It is spoken *Vachan bola* **hua**	वचन बोला **था** - I had spoken *Vachan bola* **tha**

Future And Immediate Future	Immediate Past Future
वचन बोलूँगा - I will speak *Vachan bolunga*	वचन बोलने वाला **था** - I was about to speak *Vachan bolne vala* **tha**

Imperative

Single And Polite	Future Polite
वचन बोलिए- Do speak *Vachan boliye*	वचन बोलिए**गा** - Please speak *Vachan bolie**ga***

Subjunctive

Present	Habitual And Continuous
वचन बोला **करूँ** - Do I speak *Vachan bola karun*	वचन बोला करता **हूँ** - I speak *Vachan bola karta **hun***

Perfect And Immediate Future
वचन बोलूँ- I have spoken *Vachan bolun*

Conditional

Present And Habitual	Continuous And Preterite
वचन बोलता - He speaks *Vachan bolta*	वचन बोल रहा **होता** - He would be speaking *Vachan bol raha **hota***

Presumptive

Present And Imperfective	Continuous And Future Perfect
वचन बोलता **हूँगा** – I would be speaking. *Vachan bolta **hunga***	वचन बोल रहा **हूँगा**- I would have been speaking. *Vachan bol raha **hunga***

Infinitive	To Stand	खड़ा होना *Khada hona*

Indicative

Present	Past
खड़ा होता **हूँ** - I stand *Khada hota **hun***	खड़ा होता **था** - I stood *Khada hota **tha***

Preterite And Perfect	Pluperfect
खड़ा **हुआ** - It stood *Khada **hua***	खड़ा हुआ **था** - I had stood *Khada hua **tha***

Future And Immediate Future	Immediate Past Future
खड़ा हूंगा - I will stand *Khada hunga*	खड़ा हो वाला **था** - I was about to stand *Khada horne vala **tha***

Imperative	

Single And Polite	Future Polite
खड़े हुआ **करिए** - Do stand *Khada* करिए	खड़े होइएगा - Please stand *Khada kijie**ga***

Subjunctive	

Present	Habitual And Continuous
खड़ा **होऊँ** - Do I stand *Khada houn*	खड़ा होता **हूँ** - I stand *Khada karta* **hun**

Perfect And Immediate Future
खड़ा हुआ **हूँ** - I have stood *Khada huahun*

Conditional

Present And Habitual	Continuous And Preterite
खड़ा **होता** - He stands *Khada hota*	खड़ा रहा **होता** - He would be standing *Khada raha hota*

Presumptive

Present And Imperfective	Continuous And Future Perfect
खड़ा **हूँगा** – I would be standing. *Khada hunga*	खड़ा रहा **हूँगा**- I would have been standing. *Khada raha hunga*

Infinitive	To Start	आरंभ करना *Aarambha karna*

Indicative

Present	Past
आरंभ करता **हूँ** - I start *Aarambha karta **hun***	आरंभ करता **था** - I started *Aarambha karta **tha***

Preterite And Perfect	Pluperfect
आरंभ किया **हुआ** - It is started *Aarambha kiya **hua***	आरंभ किया **था** - I had started *Aarambha kiya **tha***

Future And Immediate Future	Immediate Past Future
आरंभ क**रूँगा** - I will start *Aarambha karu**nga***	आरंभ करने वाला **था** - I was about to start *Aarambha karne vala **tha***

Imperative

Single And Polite	Future Polite
आरंभ **करिए** - Do start *Aarambha kariye*	आरंभ कीजिएगा - Please start *Aarambha kijiega*

Subjunctive

Present	Habitual And Continuous
आरंभ **करूँ** – Do I start *Aarambha karun*	आरंभ करता हूँ - I start *Aarambha karta hun*

Perfect And Immediate Future
आरंभ किया है - I have started *Aarambha kiya hai hun*

Conditional

Present And Habitual	Continuous And Preterite
आरंभ **करता** - He starts *Aarambha karta*	आरंभ कर रहा **होता** - He would be starting *Aarambha **kar** raha **hota***

Presumptive

Present And Imperfective	Continuous And Future Perfect
आरंभ करता **हूँगा** – I would be starting. *Aarambha karta **hunga***	आरंभ कर रहा **हूँगा**- I would have been starting. *Aarambha **kar** raha **hunga***

Infinitive	To Stay	ठहरना *Thaharna*

Indicative

Present	Past
ठहरता **हूँ** - I stay *Thaharta hun*	ठहरता **था** - I stayed *Thaharta tha*

Preterite And Perfect	Pluperfect
ठहरा **हुआ** - It is stayed *Thahara hua*	ठहरा **था** - I had stayed *Thahara tha*

Future And Immediate Future	Immediate Past Future
ठहरूँगा - I will stay *Thaharunga*	ठहरने वाला **था** - I was about to stay *Thaharne vala tha*

Imperative

Single And Polite	Future Polite
ठहरिए - Do stay *Tha*hariye	ठहरिए**गा** - Please stay *Tha*harie**ga**

Subjunctive

Present	Habitual And Continuous
ठहरूँ - Do I stay *Tha*harun	ठहरता हूँ - I stay *Tha*harta **hun**

Perfect And Immediate Future
ठहरा हूँ - I have stayed *Tha*hara **hun**

Conditional	

Present And Habitual	Continuous And Preterite
ठहरता - He stays *Thaharta*	ठहर रहा **होता** - He would be staying *Thahar raha* **hota**

Presumptive	

Present And Imperfective	Continuous And Future Perfect
ठहरता **हूँगा** – I would be staying. *Thaharta* **hunga**	ठहर रहा **हूँगा**- I would have been staying. *Thahar raha* **hunga**

Infinitive	To Take	लेना *Lena*

Indicative

Present	Past
लेता हूँ - I take *Leta **hun***	लेता **था** - I took *Leta **tha***

Preterite And Perfect	Pluperfect
लिया **हुआ** - It is taken *Liya **hua***	लिया **था** - I had taken *Liya **tha***

Future And Immediate Future	Immediate Past Future
लूँगा- I will take *Lunga*	लेने वाला **था** - I was about to take *Lene vala **tha***

Imperative

Single And Polite	Future Polite
लीजिये - Do take *Leejiye*	लीजिएगा - Please take *Leejiega*

Subjunctive

Present	Habitual And Continuous
लूँ - Do I take *Lun*	लेता हूँ - I take *Leta hun*

Perfect And Immediate Future
लिया हूँ - I have taken *Liya hun*

Conditional

Present And Habitual	Continuous And Preterite
लेता - He takes Leta	ले रहा **होता** - He would be taking Le raha **hota**

Presumptive

Present And Imperfective	Continuous And Future Perfect
लेता **हूँगा** – I would be taking. Leta **hunga**	ले रहा **हूँगा**- I would have been taking. Le raha **hunga**

Infinitive	To Talk	वार्तालाप करना *Vartalaap karna*

Indicative

Present	Past
वार्तालाप करता हूँ - I talk *Vartalaap karta **hun***	वार्तालाप करता **था** - I talked *Vartalaap karta **tha***

Preterite And Perfect	Pluperfect
वार्तालाप किया **हुआ** - It is talked *Vartalaap kiya **hua***	वार्तालाप किया **था** - I had talked *Vartalaap kiya **tha***

Future And Immediate Future	Immediate Past Future
वार्तालाप करूँगा - I will talk *Vartalaap karu**nga***	वार्तालाप करने वाला **था** - I was about to talk *Vartalaap karne vala **tha***

Imperative

Single And Polite	Future Polite
वार्तालाप **करिए** - Do talk *Vartalaap **kariye***	वार्तालाप कीजिए**गा** - Please talk *Vartalaap kijie**ga***

Subjunctive

Present	Habitual And Continuous
वार्तालाप **करूँ** - Do I talk *Vartalaap karun*	वार्तालाप करता हूँ - I talk *Vartalaap karta **hun***

Perfect And Immediate Future
वार्तालाप करा हूँ - I have talked *Vartalaap kara **hun***

Conditional

Present And Habitual	Continuous And Preterite
वार्तालाप **करता** - He talks *Vartalaap karta*	वार्तालाप कर रहा **होता** - He would be talking *Vartalaap **kar** raha **hota***

Presumptive

Present And Imperfective	Continuous And Future Perfect
वार्तालाप करता **हूँगा** – I would be talking. *Vartalaap karta **hunga***	वार्तालाप कर रहा **हूँगा**- I would have been talking. *Vartalaap **kar** raha **hunga***

Infinitive	To Teach	शिक्षित करना *Shikshit karna*

Indicative

Present	Past
शिक्षित करता हूँ - I teach *Shikshit karta **hun***	शिक्षित करता **था** - I taught *Shikshit karta **tha***

Preterite And Perfect	Pluperfect
शिक्षित किया **हुआ** - It is taught *Shikshit kiya **hua***	शिक्षित किया **था** - I had taught *Shikshit kiya **tha***

Future And Immediate Future	Immediate Past Future
शिक्षित करूँगा - I will teach *Shikshit karu**nga***	शिक्षित करने वाला **था** - I was about to teach *Shikshit karne vala **tha***

Imperative

Single And Polite	Future Polite
शिक्षित **करिए** - Do teach Shikshit **kariye**	शिक्षित कीजिए**गा** - Please teach Shikshit kijie**ga**

Subjunctive

Present	Habitual And Continuous
शिक्षित **करूँ** - Do I teach Shikshit **karun**	शिक्षित करता **हूँ** - I teach Shikshit karta **hun**

Perfect And Immediate Future
शिक्षित किया है - I have taught   Shikshit kiya hai

Conditional	
Present And Habitual	**Continuous And Preterite**
शिक्षित **करता** - He teachs *Shikshit karta*	शिक्षित कर रहा **होता** - He would be teaching *Shikshit **kar** raha **hota***

Presumptive	
Present And Imperfective	**Continuous And Future Perfect**
शिक्षित करता **हूँगा** – I would be teaching. *Shikshit karta **hunga***	शिक्षित कर रहा **हूँगा**- I would have been teaching. *Shikshit **kar** raha **hunga***

Infinitive	To Think	विचार करना *Vichaar karna*

Indicative

Present	Past
विचार करता **हूँ** - I think *Vichaar karta* **hun**	विचार करता **था** - I thought *Vichaar karta* **tha**

Preterite And Perfect	Pluperfect
विचार किया **हुआ** - It is thought *Vichaar kiya* **hua**	विचार किया **था** - I had thought *Vichaar kiya* **tha**

Future And Immediate Future	Immediate Past Future
विचार करूँ**गा** - I will think *Vichaar karunga*	विचार करने वाला **था** - I was about to think *Vichaar karne vala* **tha**

Imperative

Single And Polite	Future Polite
विचार **करिए** - Do think *Vichaar **kariye***	विचार कीजिए**गा** - Please think *Vichaar kijie**ga***

Subjunctive

Present	Habitual And Continuous
विचार **करूँ** - Do I think *Vichaar karun*	विचार करता **हूँ** - I think *Vichaar karta **hun***

Perfect And Immediate Future
विचार किया है - I have thought *Vichaar kiya hai*

Conditional

Present And Habitual	Continuous And Preterite
विचार **करता** - He thinks *Vichaar karta*	विचार कर रहा **होता** - He would be thinking *Vichaar **kar** raha **hota***

Presumptive

Present And Imperfective	Continuous And Future Perfect
विचार करता **हूँगा** – I would be thinking. *Vichaar karta **hunga***	विचार कर रहा **हूँगा**- I would have been thinking. *Vichaar **kar** raha **hunga***

Infinitive	To Touch	छूना *Chhuna*

Indicative

Present	Past
छूता हूँ - I touch *Chhuta hun*	छूता **था** - I touched *Chhuta tha*

Preterite And Perfect	Pluperfect
छुआ **हुआ** - It is touched *Chhua hua*	छुआ **था** - I had touched *Chhuya tha*

Future And Immediate Future	Immediate Past Future
छूऊंगा - I will touch *Chhuonga*	छूने वाला **था** - I was about to touch *Chhune vala tha*

Imperative

Single And Polite	Future Polite
छूईए - Do touch	छूईएगा - Please touch
Chhueeye	*Chhuiega*

Subjunctive

Present	Habitual And Continuous
छूऊँ - Do I touch	छूता हूँ - I touch
Chhuun	*Chhuta hun*

Perfect And Immediate Future
छुआ है - I have touched
Chhua hai

Conditional	

Present And Habitual	Continuous And Preterite
छूता - He touches *Chhuta*	छू रहा **होता** - He would be touching *Chhu raha* **hota**

Presumptive	

Present And Imperfective	Continuous And Future Perfect
छूता **हूँगा** – I would be touching. *Chhuta* **hunga**	छू रहा **हूँगा**- I would have been touching. *Chhu raha* **hunga**

Infinitive	To Travel	भ्रमण करना *Bhraman karna*

Indicative		

Present	Past
भ्रमण करता हूँ - I travel *Bhraman karta hun*	भ्रमण करता **था** - I travelled *Bhraman karta tha*

Preterite And Perfect	Pluperfect
भ्रमण किया **हुआ** - It is travelled *Bhraman kiya hua*	भ्रमण किया **था** - I had travelled *Bhraman kiya tha*

Future And Immediate Future	Immediate Past Future
भ्रमण करूँगा - I will travel *Bhraman karunga*	भ्रमण करने वाला **था** - I was about to travel *Bhraman karne vala tha*

Imperative

Single And Polite	Future Polite
भ्रमण **करिए** - Do travel *Bhraman **kariye***	भ्रमण कीजिए**गा** - Please travel *Bhraman kijie**ga***

Subjunctive

Present	Habitual And Continuous
भ्रमण **करूँ** - Do I travel *Bhraman karun*	भ्रमण करता हूँ - I travel *Bhraman karta **hun***

Perfect And Immediate Future
भ्रमण करा हूँ - I have travelled *Bhraman kara **hun***

Conditional

Present And Habitual	Continuous And Preterite
भ्रमण **करता** - He travels *Bhraman karta*	भ्रमण कर रहा **होता** - He would be travelling *Bhraman **kar** raha **hota***

Presumptive

Present And Imperfective	Continuous And Future Perfect
भ्रमण करता **हूँगा** – I would be travelling. *Bhraman karta **hunga***	भ्रमण कर रहा **हूँगा**- I would have been travelling. *Bhraman **kar** raha **hunga***

Infinitive	To Understand	समझना *Samajhna*

	Indicative	

Present	Past
समझता हूँ - I understand *Samajhta* **hun**	समझता **था** - I understood *Samajhta* **tha**

Preterite And Perfect	Pluperfect
समझा **हुआ** - It is understood *Samajha* **hua**	समझा **था** - I had understood *Samajha* **tha**

Future And Immediate Future	Immediate Past Future
समझा करूँगा - I will understand *Samajha karunga*	समझने वाला **था** - I was about to understand *Samajhne vala* **tha**

Imperative

Single And Polite	Future Polite
समझिए - Do understand *Samajhiye*	समझिएगा - Please understand *Samajhjie**ga***

Subjunctive

Present	Habitual And Continuous
समझूँ - Do I understand *Samaj**hun***	समझता हूँ - I understand *Samajhta **hun***

Perfect And Immediate Future
समझा हूँ - I have understood *Samajha **hun***

Conditional	
Present And Habitual	**Continuous And Preterite**
समझता - He understands *Samajhta*	समझ रहा **होता** - He would be understanding *Samajh **kar** raha **hota***

Presumptive	
Present And Imperfective	**Continuous And Future Perfect**
समझता **हूँगा** – I would be understanding. *Samajhta **hunga***	समझ रहा **हूँगा**- I would have been understanding. *Samajh raha **hunga***

Infinitive	To Use	उपयोग करना *Upayog karna*

Indicative

Present	Past
उपयोग करता **हूँ** - I use *Upayog karta* **hun**	उपयोग करता **था** - I used *Upayog karta* **tha**

Preterite And Perfect	Pluperfect
उपयोग किया **हुआ** - It is used *Upayog kiya* **hua**	उपयोग किया **था** - I had used *Upayog kiya* **tha**

Future And Immediate Future	Immediate Past Future
उपयोग कर**रूँगा** - I will use *Upayog karun***ga**	उपयोग करने वाला **था** - I was about to use *Upayog karne vala* **tha**

Imperative

Single And Polite	Future Polite
उपयोग **करिए** - Do use Upayog **kariye**	उपयोग कीजिए**गा** - Please use Upayog kijie**ga**

Subjunctive

Present	Habitual And Continuous
उपयोग **करूँ** - Do I use Upayog **karun**	उपयोग करता **हूँ** - I use Upayog karta **hun**

Perfect And Immediate Future
उपयोग किया है - I have used Upayog kiya hai

Conditional

Present And Habitual	Continuous And Preterite
उपयोग **करता** - He uses *Upayog karta*	उपयोग कर रहा **होता** - He would be using *Upayog **kar** raha **hota***

Presumptive

Present And Imperfective	Continuous And Future Perfect
उपयोग करता **हूँगा** – I would be using. *Upayog karta **hunga***	उपयोग कर रहा **हूँगा**- I would have been using. *Upayog **kar** raha **hunga***

Infinitive	To Wait	प्रतीक्षा करना
		Prateeksha karna

Indicative

Present	Past
प्रतीक्षा करता हूँ - I wait *Prateeksha karta* **hun**	प्रतीक्षा करता **था** - I waited *Prateeksha karta* **tha**

Preterite And Perfect	Pluperfect
प्रतीक्षा किया **हुआ** - It is waited *Prateeksha kiya* **hua**	प्रतीक्षा किया **था** - I had waited *Prateeksha kiya* **tha**

Future And Immediate Future	Immediate Past Future
प्रतीक्षा करूँगा - I will wait *Prateeksha karun***ga**	प्रतीक्षा करने वाला **था** - I was about to wait *Prateeksha karne vala* **tha**

177

Imperative

Single And Polite	Future Polite
प्रतीक्षा **करिए** - Do wait Prateeksha **kariyega**	प्रतीक्षा कीजिए**गा** - Please wait Prateeksha kijie**ga**

Subjunctive

Present	Habitual And Continuous
प्रतीक्षा **करूँ** - Do I wait Prateeksha karun	प्रतीक्षा करता **हूँ** - I wait Prateeksha karta **hun**

Perfect And Immediate Future
प्रतीक्षा की है - I have waited Prateeksha kee hai **hun**

Conditional

Present And Habitual	Continuous And Preterite
प्रतीक्षा **करता** - He waits *Prateeksha karta*	प्रतीक्षा कर रहा **होता** - He would be waiting *Prateeksha **kar** raha **hota***

Presumptive

Present And Imperfective	Continuous And Future Perfect
प्रतीक्षा करता **हूँगा** – I would be waiting. *Prateeksha karta **hunga***	प्रतीक्षा कर रहा **हूँगा**- I would have been waiting. *Prateeksha **kar** raha **hunga***

Infinitive	To Want	मन करना *Man karna*

Indicative

Present	Past
मन करता **है** - I want *Man karta **hai***	मन करता **था** - I wanted *Man karta **tha***

Preterite And Perfect	Pluperfect
मन किया **हुआ** - It is wanted *Man kiya **hua***	मन किया **था** - I had wanted *Man kiya **tha***

Future And Immediate Future	Immediate Past Future
मन करेगा - I will want *Man karega*	मन करने वाला **था** - I was about to want *Man karne vala **tha***

Imperative

Single And Polite	Future Polite
मन कीजिये - Do want *Man keejiye*	मन कीजिएगा - Please want *Man kijiega*

Subjunctive

Present	Habitual And Continuous
मन करे - Do I want *Man kare*	मन करता है - I want *Man karta hai*

Perfect And Immediate Future
मन किया है - I have wanted *Man kiya hai*

Conditional

Present And Habitual	Continuous And Preterite
मन **करता** - He wants Man karta	मन कर रहा **होता** - He would be wanting Man **kar** raha **hota**

Presumptive

Present And Imperfective	Continuous And Future Perfect
मन करता **होगा** – I would be wanting. Man karta **hoga**	मन कर रहा होगा- I would have been wanting. Man **kar** raha **hoga**

| Infinitive | To Watch | देखना

Dekhna |
| --- | --- | --- |

Indicative

Present	Past
देखता हूँ - I watch

Dekhta hun | देखता **था** - I watched

Dekhta tha |

Preterite And Perfect	Pluperfect
देखा **हुआ** - It is watched

Dekha hua | देखा **था** - I had watched

Dekha tha |

Future And Immediate Future	Immediate Past Future
देखूंगा - I will watch

Dekhunga | देखने वाला **था** - I was about to watch

Dekhne vala tha |

Imperative

Single And Polite	Future Polite
देखिए - Do watch *Dekhiye*	देखिएगा - Please watch *Dekhie**ga***

Subjunctive

Present	Habitual And Continuous
देखा करूँ - Do I watch *Dekha karun*	देखता हूँ - I watch *Dekhta **hun***

Perfect And Immediate Future
देखा है - I have watched *Dekha hai*

Conditional

Present And Habitual	Continuous And Preterite
देखता - He watches Dekhta	देख रहा **होता** - He would be watching Dekh raha **hota**

Presumptive

Present And Imperfective	Continuous And Future Perfect
देखता **हूँगा** – I would be watching. Dekhta **hunga**	देख रहा **हूँगा**- I would have been watching. Dekh raha **hunga**

Infinitive	To Win	जीतना *Jeetana*

Indicative

Present	Past
जीतता - I win *Jeetata **hun***	जीतता **था** - I won *Jeet**tha***

Preterite And Perfect	Pluperfect
जीता **हुआ** - It is won *Jeeta **hua***	जीता था - I had won *Jeeta **tha***

Future And Immediate Future	Immediate Past Future
जीतूंगा - I will win *Jeetunga*	जीतने वाला **था** - I was about to win *Jeetane vala **tha***

Imperative

Single And Polite	Future Polite
जीतिए - Do win *Jeetiye*	जीतिएगा - Please win *Jeetiega*

Subjunctive

Present	Habitual And Continuous
जीतूँ - Do I win *Jeetun*	जीतता हूँ - I win *Jeetata hun*

Perfect And Immediate Future
जीता हूँ - I have won *Jeeta hun*

Conditional

Present And Habitual	Continuous And Preterite
जीतता - He wins Jeetata	जीत रहा **होता** - He would be winning Jeet raha **hota**

Presumptive

Present And Imperfective	Continuous And Future Perfect
जीतता **हूँगा** – I would be winning. Jeetata **hunga**	जीतता रहाहूँगा- I would have been winning. Jeeta **hunga**

Infinitive	To Work	कार्य करना *Kaarya karna*

Indicative

Present	Past
कार्य करता हूँ - I work *Kaarya karta* **hun**	कार्य करता **था** - I worked *Kaarya karta* **tha**

Preterite And Perfect	Pluperfect
कार्य किया **हुआ** - It is worked *Kaarya kiya* **hua**	कार्य किया **था** - I had worked *Kaarya kiya* **tha**

Future And Immediate Future	Immediate Past Future
कार्य करूँगा - I will work *Kaarya karun***ga**	कार्य करने वाला **था** - I was about to work *Kaarya karne vala* **tha**

Imperative

Single And Polite	Future Polite
कार्य **करिए** - Do work Kaarya **kariye**	कार्य कीजिए**गा** - Please work Kaarya kijie**ga**

Subjunctive

Present	Habitual And Continuous
कार्य **करूँ** - Do I work Kaarya **karun**	कार्य करता **हूँ** - I work Kaarya karta **hun**

Perfect And Immediate Future
कार्य किया है - I have worked Kaarya kiya hai

Conditional

Present And Habitual	Continuous And Preterite
कार्य **करता** - He works *Kaarya karta*	कार्य कर रहा **होता** - He would be working *Kaarya **kar** raha **hota***

Presumptive

Present And Imperfective	Continuous And Future Perfect
कार्य करता **हूँगा** – I would be working. *Kaarya karta **hunga***	कार्य कर रहा **हूँगा**- I would have been working. *Kaarya **kar** raha **hunga***

Infinitive	To Write	लिखना *Likhna*

Indicative

Present	Past
लिखता हूँ - I write *Likhta **hun***	लिखता **था** - I wrote *Likhta **tha***

Preterite And Perfect	Pluperfect
लिखा **हुआ** - It is written *Likha **hua***	लिखा **था** - I had written *Likha **tha***

Future And Immediate Future	Immediate Past Future
लिख करूँगा - I will write *Likhunga*	लिखने वाला **था** - I was about to write *Likhne vala **tha***

Imperative

Single And Polite	Future Polite
लिखिए - Do write *Likhiye*	लिखिएगा - Please write *Likhiega*

Subjunctive

Present	Habitual And Continuous
लिखा करूँ - Do I write *Likhun*	लिखता हूँ - I write *Likhta hun*

Perfect And Immediate Future
लिखा है - I have written *Likha hai*

Conditional

Present And Habitual	Continuous And Preterite
लिखता - He writes *Likhta*	लिख रहा **होता** - He would be writing *Likh raha **hota***

Presumptive

Present And Imperfective	Continuous And Future Perfect
लिखता **हूँगा** – I would be writing. *Likhta **hunga***	लिख रहा **हूँगा**- I would have been writing. *Likh raha **hunga***

Infinitive	To meet	मिलना *Milna*

Indicative

Present	Past
मिलता **हूँ** - I meet *Milta*	मिलता **था** - I met *Milta* **tha**

Preterite And Perfect	Pluperfect
मिला **हुआ** - It is met *Mila* **hua**	मिला **था** - I had met *Mila* **tha**

Future And Immediate Future	Immediate Past Future
मिलूँगा - I will meet *Milunga*	मिलने वाला **था** - I was about to meet *Milane vala* **tha**

Imperative

Single And Polite	Future Polite
मिलिए - Do meet Miliye	मिलिएगा - Please meet Milie**ga**

Subjunctive

Present	Habitual And Continuous
मिलूँ - Do I meet Milun	मिलता हूँ - I meet Milta **hun**

Perfect And Immediate Future
मिला हूँ - I have met Mila**hun**

Conditional	

Present And Habitual	Continuous And Preterite
मिलता - He meets Milta	मिल रहा **होता** - He would be meeting Mil raha **hota**

Presumptive	

Present And Imperfective	Continuous And Future Perfect
मिल रहता होता – I would be meeting. Mila rahta **hota**	मिल रहा **हूँगा**- I would have been meeting. Mila raha **hunga**

Infinitive	To Need	आवश्यकता होना
		Avashayakta होना

Indicative

Present	Past
आवश्यकता है - I need	आवश्यकता थी- I needed
Avashayakta hai	*Avashayakta* **thee**

Preterite And Perfect	Pluperfect
आवश्यकता हुई हैhai - It is needed	आवश्यकता हुई थी - I had needed
Avashayakta hui hai	*Avashayakta huiee thee*

Future And Immediate Future	Immediate Past Future
आवश्यकता होगी - I will need	आवश्यकता होने वाली थी - I was about to need
Avashayakta hogee	*Avashayakta hone valee thee*

Imperative

Single And Polite	Future Polite
आवश्यकता **बनाइये** - Do need *Avashayakta banaeeye*	आवश्यकता बनाईएग**गा** - Please need *Avashayakta banaiyega*

Subjunctive

Present	Habitual And Continuous
आवश्यकता है - Do I need *Avashayakta hai*	आवश्यकता होती रहती है - I need *Avashayakta hotee rahtee hai*

Perfect And Immediate Future
आवश्यकता हुई है - I have needed *Avashayakta **hui hai***

Conditional

Present And Habitual	Continuous And Preterite
आवश्यकता होती - He needs *Avashayakta hotee*	आवश्यकता हो रही होती है - He would be needing *Avashayakta ho rahee hotee hai*

Presumptive

Present And Imperfective	Continuous And Future Perfect
आवश्यकता होगी – I would be needing. *Avashayakta hogee*	आवश्यकता हो रही होगी- I would have been needing. *Avashayakta ho rahee hogee*

Infinitive	To Notice	ध्यान देना *Dhyaan dena*

Indicative

Present	Past
ध्यान देता हूँ - I notice *Dhyaan deta **hun***	ध्यान देता **था** - I noticed *Dhyaan deta **tha***

Preterite And Perfect	Pluperfect
ध्यान दिया **हुआ** - It is noticed *Dhyaan diya **hua***	ध्यान दिया **था** - I had noticed *Dhyaan diya **tha***

Future And Immediate Future	Immediate Past Future
ध्यान दूँगा - I will notice *Dhyaan dun**ga***	ध्यान देने वाला **था** - I was about to notice *Dhyaan dene vala **tha***

Imperative

Single And Polite	Future Polite
ध्यान दीजिये - Do notice *Dhyaan deejiye*	ध्यान दीजिएगा - Please notice *Dhyaan dijie**ga***

Subjunctive

Present	Habitual And Continuous
ध्यान दूँ - Do I notice *Dhyaan dun*	ध्यान देता हूँ - I notice *Dhyaan deta **hun***

Perfect And Immediate Future
ध्यान दिया है - I have noticed *Dhyaan diya hai*

Conditional

Present And Habitual	Continuous And Preterite
ध्यान देता - He notices *Dhyaan deta*	ध्यान दे रहा **होता** - He would be noticing *Dhyaan de raha **hota***

Presumptive

Present And Imperfective	Continuous And Future Perfect
ध्यान देता **हूँगा** – I would be noticing. *Dhyaan deta **hunga***	ध्यान दे रहा **हूँगा**- I would have been noticing. *Dhyaan de raha **hunga***

Infinitive	To Open	खोलना *Kholna*

Indicative

Present	Past
खोलता हूँ - I open *Kholta* **hun**	खोलता **था** - I opened *Kholta* **tha**

Preterite And Perfect	Pluperfect
खोला **हुआ** - It is opened *Khola* **hua**	खोला **था** - I had opened *Khola* **tha**

Future And Immediate Future	Immediate Past Future
खोलूँगा - I will open *Khola karunga*	खोलने वाला **था** - I was about to open *Kholne vala* **tha**

Imperative

Single And Polite	Future Polite
खोलिए - Do open *Kholiye*	खोलिएगा - Please open *Kholiega*

Subjunctive

Present	Habitual And Continuous
खोलूँ - Do I open *Kholun*	खोलता हूँ - I open *Kholta hun*

Perfect And Immediate Future
खोला हूँ - I have opened *Khola hun*

Conditional

Present And Habitual	Continuous And Preterite
खोलता - He opens *Kholta*	खोल रहा **होता** - He would be opening *Khol raha **hota***

Presumptive

Present And Imperfective	Continuous And Future Perfect
खोलता **हूँगा** – I would be opening. *Kholta **hunga***	खोल रहा **हूँगा**- I would have been opening. *Khol raha **hunga***

Infinitive	To Play	खेलना *Khelna*

Indicative

Present	Past
खेलता हूँ - I play *Khelta* **hun**	खेलता **था** - I played *Khelta* **tha**

Preterite And Perfect	Pluperfect
खेला **हुआ** - It is played *Khela* **hua**	खेला **था** - I had played *Khela* **tha**

Future And Immediate Future	Immediate Past Future
खेलूँगा - I will play *Khelunga*	खेलने वाला **था** - I was about to play *Khelne vala* **tha**

Imperative

Single And Polite	Future Polite
खेलिए - Do play *Kheliye*	खेलिएगा - Please play *Kheliega*

Subjunctive

Present	Habitual And Continuous
खेला करूँ - Do I play *Khela karun*	खेलता हूँ - I play *Khelta hun*

Perfect And Immediate Future
खेला हूँ - I have played *Khela hun*

Conditional

Present And Habitual	Continuous And Preterite
खेलता - He plays *Khelata*	खेल रहा **होता** - He would be playing *Khel raha* **hota**

Presumptive

Present And Imperfective	Continuous And Future Perfect
खेलता **हूँगा** – I would be playing. *Khelata* **hunga**	खेल रहा **हूँगा**- I would have been playing. *Khel* **kar** *raha* **hunga**

Infinitive	To Put	रखना
		Rakhna

Indicative

Present	Past
रखता हूँ - I put	रखता **था** - I put
Rakhta **hun**	*Rakhta* **tha**

Preterite And Perfect	Pluperfect
रखा **हुआ** - It is put	रखा **था** - I had put
Rakha **hua**	*Rakha* **tha**

Future And Immediate Future	Immediate Past Future
रखूँगा - I will put	रखने वाला **था** - I was about to put
Rakhunga	*Rakhne vala* **tha**

Imperative

Single And Polite	Future Polite
रखिए - Do put *Rakhiye*	रखिएगा - Please put *Rakhiega*

Subjunctive

Present	Habitual And Continuous
रखा करूँ – Do I put *Rakha karun*	रखा करता हूँ - I put *Rakha karta hun*

Perfect And Immediate Future
रखा है - I have put *Rakha hai*

Conditional

Present And Habitual	Continuous And Preterite
रखता - He puts Rakhta	रख रहा **होता** - He would be putting Rakh raha **hota**

Presumptive

Present And Imperfective	Continuous And Future Perfect
रखता **हूँगा** – I would be putting. Rakhta **hunga**	रख रहा **हूँगा** - I would have been putting. Rakh raha **hunga**

Infinitive	To Read	पढ़ना *Padhna*

Indicative

Present	Past
पढ़ता **हूँ** - I read *Padhta* **hun**	पढ़ता **था** - I read *Padhta* **tha**

Preterite And Perfect	Pluperfect
पढ़ा **हुआ** - It is read *Padha* **hua**	पढ़ा **था** - I had read *Padha* **tha**

Future And Immediate Future	Immediate Past Future
पढ़ा करूँगा - I will read *Padha karunga*	पढ़ने वाला **था** - I was about to read *Padhne vala* **tha**

Imperative

Single And Polite	Future Polite
पढ़िए - Do read Padhiye	पढ़िएगा - Please read Padhiega

Subjunctive

Present	Habitual And Continuous
पढ़ूँ - Do I read Padhun	पढ़ता हूँ - I read Padta hun

Perfect And Immediate Future
पढ़ा हूँ - I have read Padha hun

Conditional

Present And Habitual	Continuous And Preterite
पढ़ता - He reads *Padhta*	पढ़ रहा **होता** - He would be reading *Padh raha **hota***

Presumptive

Present And Imperfective	Continuous And Future Perfect
पढ़ता **हूँगा** – I would be reading. *Padhta **hunga***	पढ़ रहा **हूँगा**- I would have been reading. *Padh raha **hunga***

Infinitive	To Receive	प्राप्त करना *Prapt karna*

Indicative

Present	Past
प्राप्त करता हूँ - I receive *Prapt karta* **hun**	प्राप्त करता **था** - I received *Prapt karta* **tha**

Preterite And Perfect	Pluperfect
प्राप्त किया **हुआ** - It is received *Prapt kiya* **hua**	प्राप्त किया **था** - I had received *Prapt kiya* **tha**

Future And Immediate Future	Immediate Past Future
प्राप्त करूँगा - I will receive *Prapt karunga*	प्राप्त करने वाला **था** - I was about to receive *Prapt karne vala* **tha**

Imperative

Single And Polite	Future Polite
प्राप्त **करिए** - Do receive	प्राप्त कीजिए**गा** - Please receive
*Prapt **kariye***	*Prapt kijie**ga***

Subjunctive

Present	Habitual And Continuous
प्राप्त **करूँ** - Do I receive	प्राप्त करता **हूँ** - I receive
Prapt karun	*Prapt karta **hun***

Perfect And Immediate Future
प्राप्त किया है - I have received
Prapt kiya hai

Conditional

Present And Habitual	Continuous And Preterite
प्राप्त **करता** - He receives *Prapt karta*	प्राप्त कर रहा **होता** - He would be receiving *Prapt **kar** raha **hota***

Presumptive

Present And Imperfective	Continuous And Future Perfect
प्राप्त करता **हूँगा** – I would be receiving. *Prapt karta **hunga***	प्राप्त कर रहा **हूँगा**- I would have been receiving. *Prapt **kar** raha **hunga***

Infinitive	To Remember	याद करना
		Yaad karna

Indicative

Present	Past
याद करता **हूँ** - I remember	याद करता **था** - I remembered
Yaad karta **hun**	*Yaad karta* **tha**

Preterite And Perfect	Pluperfect
याद किया **हुआ** - It is remembered	याद किया **था** - I had remembered
Yaad kiya **hua**	*Yaad kiya* **tha**

Future And Immediate Future	Immediate Past Future
याद करूँगा - I will remember	याद करने वाला **था** - I was about to remember
*Yaad karu**nga***	*Yaad karne vala* **tha**

Imperative

Single And Polite	Future Polite
याद **करिए** - Do remember Yaad **kariye**	याद कीजिए**गा** - Please remember Yaad kijie**ga**

Subjunctive

Present	Habitual And Continuous
याद **करूँ** - Do I remember Yaad karun	याद करता हूँ - I remember Yaad karta **hun**

Perfect And Immediate Future
याद किया है - I have remembered Yaad kiya hai **hun**

Conditional

Present And Habitual	Continuous And Preterite
याद **करता** - He remembers *Yaad karta*	याद कर रहा **होता** - He would be remembering *Yaad **kar** raha **hota***

Presumptive

Present And Imperfective	Continuous And Future Perfect
याद करता **हूँगा** – I would be remembering. *Yaad karta **hunga***	याद कर रहा **हूँगा**- I would have been remembering. *Yaad **kar** raha **hunga***

Infinitive	To Repeat	दोबारा करना *Dobara karna*

Indicative

Present	Past
दोबारा करता **हूँ** - I repeat *Dobara karta hun*	दोबारा करता **था** - I repeated *Dobara karta tha*

Preterite And Perfect	Pluperfect
दोबारा किया **हुआ** - It is repeated *Dobara kiya hua*	दोबारा किया **था** - I had repeated *Dobara kiya tha*

Future And Immediate Future	Immediate Past Future
दोबारा करूँगा - I will repeat *Dobara karunga*	दोबारा करने वाला **था** - I was about to repeat *Dobara karne vala tha*

Imperative

Single And Polite	Future Polite
दोबारा **करिए** - Do repeat Dobara **kariye**	दोबारा कीजिएगा – Please repeat Dobara kijie**ga**

Subjunctive

Present	Habitual And Continuous
दोबारा **करूँ** – Do I repeat Dobara karun	दोबारा करता **हूँ** – I repeat Dobara karta **hun**

Perfect And Immediate Future
दोबारा करा है - I have repeated   Dobara kara **hai**

Conditional

Present And Habitual	Continuous And Preterite
दोबारा **करता** - He repeats *Dobara karta*	दोबारा कर रहा **होता** - He would be repeating *Dobara **kar** raha **hota***

Presumptive

Present And Imperfective	Continuous And Future Perfect
दोबारा करता **हूँगा** – I would be repeating. *Dobara karta **hunga***	दोबारा कर रहा **हूँगा**- I would have **been** repeating. *Dobara **kar** raha **hunga***

Infinitive	To Return	वापिस करना *Vaapis karna*

Indicative

Present	Past
वापिस करता हूँ - I return *Vaapis karta* **hun**	वापिस करता **था** - I returned *Vaapis karta* **tha**

Preterite And Perfect	Pluperfect
वापिस किया **हुआ** - It is returned *Vaapis kiya* **hua**	वापिस किया **था** - I had returned *Vaapis kiya* **tha**

Future And Immediate Future	Immediate Past Future
वापिस करूँगा - I will return *Vaapis karunga*	वापिस करने वाला **था** - I was about to return *Vaapis karne vala* **tha**

Imperative

Single And Polite	Future Polite
वापिस **करिए** - Do return *Vaapis **kariye***	वापिस कीजिए**गा** - Please return *Vaapis kijie**ga***

Subjunctive

Present	Habitual And Continuous
वापिस **करूँ** - Do I return *Vaapis karun*	वापिस करता **हूँ** - I return *Vaapis karta **hun***

Perfect And Immediate Future
वापिस किया है - I have returned *Vaapis kiya hai*

Conditional

Present And Habitual	Continuous And Preterite
वापिस **करता** - He returns *Vaapis karta*	वापिस कर रहा **होता** - He would be returning *Vaapis **kar** raha **hota***

Presumptive

Present And Imperfective	Continuous And Future Perfect
वापिस करता **हूँगा** – I would be returning. *Vaapis karta **hunga***	वापिस कर रहा **हूँगा**- I would have been returning. *Vaapis **kar** raha **hunga***

Infinitive	To Run	दौड़ना *Daudana*

Indicative

Present	Past
दौड़ता हूँ - I run *Daudata* **hun**	दौड़ता **था** - I ran *Daudata* **tha**

Preterite And Perfect	Pluperfect
दौड़ किया **हुआ** - It is run *Dauda* **hua**	दौड़ा **था** - I had run *Dauda* **tha**

Future And Immediate Future	Immediate Past Future
दौड़ा करूँगा - I will run *Dauda karunga*	दौड़ने वाला **था** - I was about to run *Daudane vala* **tha**

Imperative

Single And Polite	Future Polite
दौड़िए - Do run *Daudiye*	दौड़िएगा - Please run *Daudie**ga***

Subjunctive

Present	Habitual And Continuous
दौड़ा करूँ - Do I run *Dauda karun*	दौड़ करता हूँ - I run *Daud karta **hun***

Perfect And Immediate Future
दौड़ा हूँ - I run *Dauda **hun***

Conditional

Present And Habitual	Continuous And Preterite
दौड़ा **करता** - He runs Dauda karta	दौड़ रहा **होता** - He would be running Dauda raha **hota**

Presumptive

Present And Imperfective	Continuous And Future Perfect
दौड़ता **हूँगा** – I would be running. Daudata **hunga**	दौड़ रहा **हूँगा**- I would have been running. Dauda raha **hunga**

Infinitive	To Say	कहना *Kahana*

Indicative

Present	Past
कहता हूँ - I say *Kahata* **hun**	कहता **था** - I said *Kahata* **tha**

Preterite And Perfect	Pluperfect
कहा **हुआ** - It is said *Kaha* **hua**	कहा **था** - I had said *Kaha* **tha**

Future And Immediate Future	Immediate Past Future
कहा करूँगा - I will say *Kaha karun**ga***	कहने वाला **था** - I was about to say *Kahane vala* **tha**

Imperative

Single And Polite	Future Polite
कहिये - Do say Kahiye	कहिएगा - Please say Kahiyega

Subjunctive

Present	Habitual And Continuous
कहूँ - Do I say Kahun	कहा करता हूँ - I say Kahata **hun**

Perfect And Immediate Future
कहा है - I have said Kahaa **hai**

Conditional

Present And Habitual	Continuous And Preterite
कहा **करता** - He says *Kahata*	कह रहा **होता** - He would be saying *Kaha raha* **hota**

Presumptive

Present And Imperfective	Continuous And Future Perfect
कहता **हूँगा** – I would be saying. *Kahata* **hunga**	कह रहा **हूँगा**- I would have been saying. *Kaha raha* **hunga**

Infinitive	To Scream	चिल्लाना *Chillana*

Indicative

Present	Past
चिल्लाता हूँ - I scream *Chillata* **hun**	चिल्लाता **था** - I screamed *Chillata* **tha**

Preterite And Perfect	Pluperfect
चिल्लाया **हुआ** - It is screamed *Chillaya* **hua**	चिल्लाया **था** - I had screamed *Chillaya* **tha**

Future And Immediate Future	Immediate Past Future
चिल्लाया करूँगा - I will scream *Chillaya karunga*	चिल्लाने वाला **था** - I was about to scream *Chillane vala* **tha**

Imperative

Single And Polite	Future Polite
चिल्लाईए - Do scream Chillaiye	चिल्लाईएगा - Please scream Chillaiyega

Subjunctive

Present	Habitual And Continuous
चिल्लाया **करूँ** - Do I scream Chillaya karun	चिल्लाता **हूँ** - I scream Chillata **hun**

Perfect And Immediate Future
चिल्लाया **हूँ** - I have screamed Chillaya **hun**

Conditional

Present And Habitual	Continuous And Preterite
चिल्लाता - He screams *Chillata*	चिल्ला रहा **होता** - He would be screaming *Chilla raha **hota***

Presumptive

Present And Imperfective	Continuous And Future Perfect
चिल्लाता **हूँगा** – I would be screaming. *Chillata **hunga***	चिल्ला रहा **हूँगा**- I would have been screaming. *Chilla raha **hunga***

Infinitive	To Seem	लगना
		Lagana

Indicative

Present	Past
लगता हूँ - I seem	लगता **था** - I seemed
*Lagata***hun**	*Lagata* **tha**

Preterite And Perfect	Pluperfect
लगा - It seemed	लगा **था** - I had seemed*Laga* **tha**
Laga	

Future And Immediate Future	Immediate Past Future
लगूँगा- I will seem	लगने वाला **था** - I was about to seem
Lagoonga	*Lagane vala* **tha**

Imperative

Single And Polite	Future Polite
लगिए - Do seem *Lagiye*	लगिएगा - Please seem *Lagiyega*

Subjunctive

Present	Habitual And Continuous
लगूँ - Do I seem *Lagoon*	लगता हूँ - I seem *Lagata **hun***

Perfect And Immediate Future
लगा हूँ - I have seemed *Laga **hun***

Conditional

Present And Habitual	Continuous And Preterite
लगता - He seems *Lagataa*	लग रहा **होता** - He would be seeming *Lag raharaha **hota***

Presumptive

Present And Imperfective	Continuous And Future Perfect
लगता **हूँगा** – I would be seeming. *Lagata **hunga***	लग रहा **हूँगा**- I would have been seeming. *Lag raha **hunga***

Infinitive	To See	देखना *Dekhna*

Indicative

Present	Past
देखता हूँ - I see *Dekhta **hun***	देखता **था** - I saw *Dekhta **tha***

Preterite And Perfect	Pluperfect
देखा **हुआ** - It is saw *Dekha **hua***	देखा **था** - I had saw *Dekha **tha***

Future And Immediate Future	Immediate Past Future
देखा करूँगा - I will see *Dekha karun**ga***	देखने वाला **था** - I was about to see *Dekhne vala **tha***

Imperative

Single And Polite	Future Polite
देखिए - Do see Dekhiye	देखिएगा - Please see Dekhaiega

Subjunctive

Present	Habitual And Continuous
देखूँ - Do I see Dekhun	देखता हूँ - I see Dekhta **hun**

Perfect And Immediate Future
देखा है - I have seen Dekha **hai**

Conditional

Present And Habitual	Continuous And Preterite
देखता - He sees Dekhta	देख रहा **होता** - He would be seeing Dekh raha **hota**

Presumptive

Present And Imperfective	Continuous And Future Perfect
देखता **हूँगा** – I would be seeing. Dekhta **hunga**	देख रहा **हूँगा**- I would have been seeing. Dekh raha **hunga**

Infinitive	To Sell	बेचना
		Bechana

Indicative

Present	Past
बेचता हूँ - I sell	बेचता **था** - I sold
Bechta **hun**	*Bechta* **tha**

Preterite And Perfect	Pluperfect
बेचा **हुआ** - It is sold	बेचा **था** - I had sold
Becha **hua**	*Becha* **tha**

Future And Immediate Future	Immediate Past Future
बेचा करूँगा - I will sell	बेचने वाला **था** - I was about to sell
Becha karunga	*Bechane vala* **tha**

Imperative

Single And Polite	Future Polite
बेचा **करिए** - Do sell Becha **kariye**	बेचा कीजिए**गा** - Please sell Becha kijie**ga**

Subjunctive

Present	Habitual And Continuous
बेचा **करूँ** - Do I sell Becha karun	बेचता **हूँ** - I sell Bechta **hun**

Perfect And Immediate Future
बेचा है- I have sold   Becha **hai**

Conditional

Present And Habitual	Continuous And Preterite
बेचता - He sells *Bechta*	बेच रहा **होता** - He would be selling *Bech raha* **hota**

Presumptive

Present And Imperfective	Continuous And Future Perfect
बेचता **हूँगा** – I would be selling. *Bechta* **hunga**	बेच रहा **हूँगा**- I would have been selling. *Bech raha* **hunga**

Infinitive	To Send	भेजना
		Bhejana

Indicative

Present	Past
भेजता हूँ - I send	भेजता **था** - I sent
*Bhejata **hun***	*Bhejata **tha***

Preterite And Perfect	Pluperfect
भेजा **हुआ** - It is sent	भेजा **था** - I had sent
*Bheja **hua***	*Bheja **tha***

Future And Immediate Future	Immediate Past Future
भेजा करूँगा - I will send	भेजने वाला **था** - I was about to send
*Bheja karun**ga***	*Bhejane vala **tha***

Imperative

Single And Polite	Future Polite
भेजा **करिए** - Do send *Bheja **kariye***	भेजा कीजिए**गा** - Please send *Bheja kije**ga***

Subjunctive

Present	Habitual And Continuous
भेजा **करूँ** - Do I send *Bheja karun*	भेजा करता **हूँ** - I send *Bheja karta **hun***

Perfect And Immediate Future
भेजा है - I have sent *Bheja **hai***

Conditional

Present And Habitual	Continuous And Preterite
भेजता - He sends *Bhejata*	भेज रहा **होता** - He would be sending *Bhej raha **hota***

Presumptive

Present And Imperfective	Continuous And Future Perfect
भेजता **हूँगा** – I would be sending. *Bhejata **hunga***	भेज रहा **हूँगा**- I would have been sending. *Bhej raha **hunga***

Infinitive	To Show	प्रदर्शित करना *Pradarshit karna*

Indicative

Present	Past
प्रदर्शित करता **हूँ** - I show *Pradarshit karta **hun***	प्रदर्शित करता **था** - I showed *Pradarshit karta **tha***

Preterite And Perfect	Pluperfect
प्रदर्शित किया **हुआ** - It is showed *Pradarshit kiya **hua***	प्रदर्शित किया **था** - I had showed *Pradarshit kiya **tha***

Future And Immediate Future	Immediate Past Future
प्रदर्शित करूँगा - I will show *Pradarshit karun**ga***	प्रदर्शित करने वाला **था** - I was about to show *Pradarshit karne vala **tha***

Imperative

Single And Polite	Future Polite
प्रदर्शित **करिए** - Do show *Pradarshit **kariye***	प्रदर्शित कीजिएगा - Please show *Pradarshit kijie**ga***

Subjunctive

Present	Habitual And Continuous
प्रदर्शित **करूँ** - Do I show *Pradarshit karun*	प्रदर्शित करता हूँ - I show *Pradarshit karta **hun***

Perfect And Immediate Future
प्रदर्शित किया है - I have showed *Pradarshit kiya hai*

Conditional

Present And Habitual	Continuous And Preterite
प्रदर्शित **करता** - He shows *Pradarshit karta*	प्रदर्शित कर रहा **होता** - He would be showing *Pradarshit **kar** raha **hota***

Presumptive

Present And Imperfective	Continuous And Future Perfect
प्रदर्शित करता **हूँगा** – I would be showing. *Pradarshit karta **hunga***	प्रदर्शित कर रहा **हूँगा**- I would have been showing. *Pradarshit **kar** raha **hunga***

Infinitive	To Sing	गाना *Gana*

Indicative

Present	Past
गाता हूँ - I sing *Gata hun*	गाता था - I sang *Gata tha*

Preterite And Perfect	Pluperfect
गाया हुआ - It is sung *Gaya hua*	गाया था - I had sung *Gaya tha*

Future And Immediate Future	Immediate Past Future
गाया करूँगा - I will sing *Gaya karunga*	गाने वाला था - I was about to sing *Gane vala tha*

Imperative

Single And Polite	Future Polite
गाईए - Do sing *Gaeeye*	गाया कीजिएगा - Please sing *Gaya kijiega*

Subjunctive

Present	Habitual And Continuous
गाया करूँ - Do I sing *Gaya karun*	गाता हूँ - I sing *Gata hun*

Perfect And Immediate Future
गाया है - I have singed *Gaya hai*

Conditional

Present And Habitual	Continuous And Preterite
गाता - He sings *Ga*ta	गा रहा **होता** - He would be singing ***Ga*** *raha* ***hota***

Presumptive

Present And Imperfective	Continuous And Future Perfect
गाता हूँगा – I would be singing. *Ga*ta **hunga**	गा रहा हूँगा- I would have been singing. ***Ga*** *raha* ***hunga***

Infinitive	To Accept	स्वीकार करना *Sweekar karna*

Indicative

Present	Past
स्वीकार करता हूँ - I accept *Sweekar karta **hun***	स्वीकार करता **था** - I accepted *Sweekar karta **tha***

Preterite And Perfect	Pluperfect
स्वीकार किया **हुआ** - It is accepted *Sweekar kiya **hua***	स्वीकार किया **था** - I had accepted *Sweekar kiya **tha***

Future And Immediate Future	Immediate Past Future
स्वीकार करूँगा - I will accept *Sweekar karu**nga***	स्वीकार करने वाला **था** - I was about to accept *Sweekar karne vala **tha***

Imperative	

Single And Polite	Future Polite
स्वीकार **करिए** - Do accept *Sweekar **kariye***	स्वीकार कीजिए**गा** - Please accept *Sweekar kijie**ga***

Subjunctive	

Present	Habitual And Continuous
स्वीकार **करूँ** - Do I accept *Sweekar karun*	स्वीकार करता **हूँ** - I accept *Sweekar karta **hun***

Perfect And Immediate Future
स्वीकार किया है - I have accepted *Sweekar kiya hai*

Conditional	

Present And Habitual	Continuous And Preterite
स्वीकार **करता** - He accepts *Sweekar karta*	स्वीकार कर रहा **होता** - He would be accepting *Sweekar **kar** raha **hota***

Presumptive	

Present And Imperfective	Continuous And Future Perfect
स्वीकार करता **हूँगा** – I would be accepting. *Sweekar karta **hunga***	स्वीकार कर रहा **हूँगा**- I would have **been** accepting. *Sweekar **kar** raha **hunga***

| Infinitive | To Admit | मानना

Mananaa |
|------------|----------|------------------|

Indicative

Present	Past
मानता हूँ - I admit

Manta **hun** | माना करता **था** - I admitted

Mana karta **tha** |

Preterite And Perfect	Pluperfect
माना **हुआ** - It is admitted

Mana **hua** | माना **था** - I had admitted

Mana **tha** |

Future And Immediaute Future	Immediate Past Future
माना करूँगा - I will admit

Mana **karun**ga | मानने वाला **था** - I was about to admit

Maanne vala **tha** |

Imperative

Single And Polite	Future Polite
माना **करिए** - Do admit *Manaa **kariye***	मान लीजिए**गा** - Please admit *Maan lijie**ga***

Subjunctive

Present	Habitual And Continuous
माना **करूँ** - Do I admit *Mana **karoo***	माना करता **हूँ** - I admit *Mana karta **hu**n*

Perfect And Immediate Future
माना **है** - I have admitted   *Manaa **hai***

Conditional	

Present And Habitual	Continuous And Preterite
मानता - He admits *Manta karta*	मान रहा **होता** - He would be admitting *Maan raha* **hota**

Presumptive	

Present And Imperfective	Continuous And Future Perfect
मानता हूँगा – I would be admitting. *Manta* **hunga**	मानता रहूँगा- I would have been admitting. *Manta rahungaa*

Infinitive	To Answer	उत्तर देना Uttar dena

Indicative

Present	Past
उत्तर देता हूँ - I answer Uttar deta **hun**	उत्तर देता **था** - I answered Uttar deta **tha**

Preterite And Perfect	Pluperfect
उत्तर दिया **हुआ** - It is answered Uttar diya **hua**	उत्तर देना **था** - I had answered Uttar dena **tha**

Future And Immediate Future	Immediate Past Future
उत्तर दूँगा - I will answer Uttar dun**ga**	उत्तर देने वाला **था** - I was about to answer Uttar dene vala **tha**

Imperative

Single And Polite	Future Polite
उत्तर दीजिए - Do answer Uttar deejiye	उत्तर दीजिएगा - Please answer Uttar dijie**ga**

Subjunctive

Present	Habitual And Continuous
उत्तर दूँ - Do I answer Uttar dun	उत्तर देता हूँ - I answer Uttar deta **hun**

Perfect And Immediate Future
उत्तर दिया है - I have answered Uttar diya **hai**

Conditional

Present And Habitual	Continuous And Preterite
उत्तर देता - He answers Uttar deta	उत्तर दिया **होता** - He would be answering Uttar diya **hota**

Presumptive

Present And Imperfective	Continuous And Future Perfect
उत्तर देता **हूँगा** – I would be answering. Uttar deta **hunga**	उत्तर दे रहा **हूँगा**- I would have been answering. Uttar de raha **hunga**

Infinitive	To Appear	प्रकट होना Prakat hona

Present	Past
प्रकट **होता हूँ** - I appear Prakat **hota hun**	प्रकट **होता था** - I appeared Prakat **hota tha**

Preterite And Perfect	Pluperfect
प्रकट **हुआ** - It is appeared Prakat **hua**	प्रकट **हुआ था** - I had appeared Prakat **hua tha**

Future And Immediate Future	Immediate Past Future
प्रकट होऊँगा- I will appear Prakat houn**ga**	प्रकट होने वाला **था** - I was about to appear Prakat hone vala **tha**

Imperative

Single And Polite	Future Polite
प्रकट होईए- Do appear Prakat hoeeye	प्रकट होईएगा - Please appear Prakat hoiyega

Subjunctive

Present	Habitual And Continuous
प्रकट हूँ - Do I appear Prakat **hu**n	प्रकट **होता हूँ** - I appear Prakat **hota hu**n

Perfect And Immediate Future
प्रकट **हुआ हूँ** - I have appeared Prakat **hua hu**n

Conditional

Present And Habitual	Continuous And Preterite
प्रकट **होता** - He appears Prakat **hota**	प्रकट हो रहा **होता** - He would be appearing Prakat ho raha **hota**

Presumptive

Present And Imperfective	Continuous And Future Perfect
प्रकट **होता हूँगा** – I would be appearing. Prakat **hota hunga**	प्रकट हो रहा **हूँगा**- I would have been appearing. Prakat ho raha **hunga**

Infinitive	To Ask	पूछना Poochhna

Indicative

Present	Past
पूछता हूँ - I ask Poochhta **hun**	पूछता **था** - I asked Poochhta **tha**

Preterite And Perfect	Pluperfect
पूछा **हुआ** - It is asked Poochha **hua**	पूछा **था** - I had asked Poochha **tha**

Future And Immediate Future	Immediate Past Future
पूछा करूँगा - I will ask Poochha karun**ga**	पूछने वाला **था** - I was about to ask Poochhne vala **tha**

Imperative

Single And Polite	Future Polite
पूछिए - Do ask Poochhiye	पूछिएगा - Please ask Poochhiegaa

Subjunctive

Present	Habitual And Continuous
पूछा करूँ - Do I ask Poochha **karoo**	पूछा करता हूँ - I ask Poochha karta **hun**

Perfect And Immediate Future
पूछा है - I have asked Poochha **hai**

Conditional

Present And Habitual	Continuous And Preterite
पूछा **करता** - He asks Poochha karta	पूछा रहा **होता** - He would be asking Poochha raha **hota**

Presumptive

Present And Imperfective	Continuous And Future Perfect
पूछा करता **हूँगा** – I would be asking. Poochha karta **hunga**	पूछ रहा **हूँगा**- I would have been asking. Poochh raha **hunga**

Infinitive	To Be	होना Hona

Indicative

Present	Past
होता हूँ - I am being **Hota hun**	होता था - I had been **Hota tha**

Preterite And Perfect	Pluperfect
हुआ - It is being **hua**	हुआ था - I had been **Hua tha**

Future And Immediate Future	Immediate Past Future
हूँगा - I will be **hunga**	होने वाला था - I was about to be Hone vala **tha**

Imperative

Single And Polite	Future Polite
होना - be hona	होईएगा - Please be hoiegaa

Subjunctive

Present	Habitual And Continuous
हूँ - Do I be hun	होता हूँ - I be Hota hun

Perfect And Immediate Future
होता हूँ - I have been Hota hun

Conditional

Present And Habitual	Continuous And Preterite
होता - He is hota	हो रहा होता - He would be Ho raha hota

Presumptive

Present And Imperfective	Continuous And Future Perfect
होता हूँगा – I would being. Hota hunga	हो रहा हूँगा- I would have been Ho raha hungaa

Infinitive	To be able of	कर पाना **Kar** pana

Indicative

Present	Past
कर पाता हूँ - I am able of **Kar** pata **hun**	कर पाता **था** - I was able of Kart paata **tha**

Preterite And Perfect	Pluperfect
कर पाया - It was been able to Kar paya	कर पाया **था** - I had been able to Kar paya **tha**

Future And Immediate Future	Immediate Past Future
कर पाऊँगा- I will be able to Kar paoonga	कर पाने वाला **था** - I was about to be able to Kar पाने vala **tha**

273

Imperative

Single And Polite	Future Polite
कर पाइए - be able of **Kar paaiye**	कर पाईयगा - Please be able of Kar paaiyega

Subjunctive

Present	Habitual And Continuous
क्या मैं **करूँ** - Am I able of Kya main **karoo**	करता हूँ - I am able of Karta **hu**n

Perfect And Immediate Future
किया हूँ - I have been able of Kiya **hun**

Conditional

Present And Habitual	Continuous And Preterite
कर पाता - He is able of Kar paata	कर पा रहा **होता** - He would been able of **Kar** paa raha **hota**

Presumptive

Present And Imperfective	Continuous And Future Perfect
कर पाता **हूँगा** – I would be able of Kar paata **hunga**	कर पा रहा **हूँगा**- I would have been be able of. **Kar** paa raha **hunga**

Infinitive	To Become	बन जाना Ban jana

Indicative

Present	Past
बन जाता हूँ - I become Ban jata **hu**n	बनता **था** - I became Bantaa **tha**

Preterite And Perfect	Pluperfect
बना **हुआ** - It is became Bana **hua**	बना **था** - I had become Bana **tha**

Future And Immediate Future	Immediate Past Future
बना करूँगा - I will become Bana karun**ga**a	बनने वाला **था** - I was about to become Banana vala **tha**

Imperative

Single And Polite	Future Polite
बनिए - become Baniye	बना कीजिएगा - Please become Banaa kijiegaa

Subjunctive

Present	Habitual And Continuous
बना करूँ - Do I become Bana **karoo**	बना करता हूँ - I become Bana karta **hun**

Perfect And Immediate Future
बना हूँ - I have became Bana **hun**

Conditional

Present And Habitual	Continuous And Preterite
बना **करता** - He becomes Bana karta	बन रहा **होता** - He would be becoming Ban raha **hota**

Presumptive

Present And Imperfective	Continuous And Future Perfect
बना करता **हूँगा** – I would be becoming. Bana karta ra**hunga**	बन रहा **हूँगा**- I would have been becoming. Ban raha **hunga**

Infinitive	To Begin	आरंभ करना
		Aarambha karna

Indicative

Present	Past
आरंभ करता हूँ - I begin	आरंभ करता **था** - I be**ga**n
Aarambha karta **hu**n	Aarambha karta **tha**

Preterite And Perfect	Pluperfect
आरंभ किया **हुआ** - It is begun	आरंभ किया **था** - I had begun
Aarambha kiya **hua**	Aarambha kiya **tha**

Future And Immediate Future	Immediate Past Future
आरंभ करूँगा - I will begin	आरंभ करने वाला **था** - I was about to begin
Aarambha karun**ga**	Aarambha karne vala **tha**

Imperative	

Single And Polite	Future Polite
आरंभ **करिए** - Do begin Aarambha **kariye**	आरंभ कीजिए**गा** - Please begin Aarambha kijie**gaa**

Subjunctive	

Present	Habitual And Continuous
आरंभ **करूँ** - Do I begin Aarambha **karoon**	आरंभ करता **हूँ** - I begin Aarambha karta **hun**

Perfect And Immediate Future
आरंभ किया है - I have begun Aarambha kiya hai

Conditional

Present And Habitual	Continuous And Preterite
आरंभ **करता** - He begins Aarambha karta	आरंभ कर रहा **होता** - He would be beginning Aarambha **kar** raha **hota**

Presumptive

Present And Imperfective	Continuous And Future Perfect
आरंभ करता **हूँगा** – I would be beginning. Aarambha karta **hunga**	आरंभ कर रहा **हूँगा**- I would have been beginning. Aarambha **kar** raha **hunga**

Infinitive	To Break	भंग करना Bhang karna

Indicative

Present	Past
भंग करता हूँ - I break Bhang karta hoon	भंग करता **था** - I broke Bhang karta tha

Preterite And Perfect	Pluperfect
भंग किया **हुआ** - It is broken Bhang kiya hua	भंग किया **था** - I had broken Bhang kiya tha

Future And Immediate Future	Immediate Past Future
भंग करूँगा - I will break Bhang karoonga	भंग करने वाला **था** - I was about to break Bhang karne vala tha

Imperative

Single And Polite	Future Polite
भंग **करिए** - Do break Bhang kariye	भंग **कीजिएगा** - Please break Bhang keejiyega

Subjunctive

Present	Habitual And Continuous
भंग **करूँ** - Do I break Bhang karoon	भंग करता हूँ - I break Bhang karta hoon

Perfect And Immediate Future
भंग किया है - I have broken Bhang kiya hai

Conditional

Present And Habitual	Continuous And Preterite
भंग **करता** है - He breaks Bhang karta hai	भंग कर रहा **होता** - He would be breaking Bhang kar raha hota

Presumptive

Present And Imperfective	Continuous And Future Perfect
भंग करता **हूँगा** – I would be breaking. Bhang karta hoonga	भंग कर रहा **हूँगा**- I would have been breaking. Bhang kar raha hoonga

Infinitive	To Breathe	साँस लेना Saans lena

Indicative

Present	Past
साँस लेता **हूँ** - I breathe Saans leta **hu**n	साँस लेता **था** - I breathed Saans leta **tha**

Preterite And Perfect	Pluperfect
साँस लिया **हुआ** - It is breathed Saans liya **hua**	साँस ली थी - I had breathed Saans lee thee

Future And Immediate Future	Immediate Past Future
साँस लूँगा - I will breathe Saans lun**ga**	साँस लेने वाला **था** - I was about to breathe Saans lene vala **tha**

Imperative

Single And Polite	Future Polite
साँस लीजिये - Do breathe Saans leejiye	साँस लीजिएगा - Please breathe Saans lijiegaa

Subjunctive

Present	Habitual And Continuous
साँस लूँ - Do I breathe Saans lun	साँस लेता हूँ - I breathe Saans leta hun

Perfect And Immediate Future
साँस ली है- I have breathed Saans lee hai

Conditional

Present And Habitual	Continuous And Preterite
साँस लेता - He breathes Saans leta	साँस ले रहा **होता** - He would be breathing Saans le raha **hota**

Presumptive

Present And Imperfective	Continuous And Future Perfect
साँस लेता **हूँगा** – I would be breathing. Saans leta ra**hunga**	साँस ले रहा **हूँगा**- I would have been breathing. Saans le raha **hungaa**

Infinitive	To Buy	खरीदना khareedana

Indicative

Present	Past
खरीदता हूँ - I buy Khareedata **hun**	खरीदता **था** - I bought Khareedata **tha**

Preterite And Perfect	Pluperfect
खरीदा **हुआ** - It is bought Khareeda **hua**	खरीदा **था** - I had bought Khareeda **tha**

Future And Immediate Future	Immediate Past Future
खरीदूंगा - I will buy Khareedun**ga**	खरीदने वाला **था** - I was about to buy Khareedane vala **tha**

Imperative

Single And Polite	Future Polite
खरीदिए - Do buy Khareediye	खरीदिएगा - Please buy Khareediega

Subjunctive

Present	Habitual And Continuous
खरीदूँ - Do I buy Khareedoon	खरीदता हूँ - I buy Khareedata hun

Perfect And Immediate Future
खरीदा है - I have bought Khareeda hai

Conditional

Present And Habitual	Continuous And Preterite
खरीदता - He buys Khareedata	खरीद रहा **होता** - He would be buying Khareed raha **hota**

Presumptive

Present And Imperfective	Continuous And Future Perfect
खरीदता **हूँगा** – I would be buying. Khareedta **hunga**	खरीद रहा **हूँगा**- I would have been buying. Khareed raha **hunga**

Infinitive	To call	आह्वाहन करना Ahwaahan karna

Indicative

Present	Past
आह्वाहन करता **हूँ** - I call Ahwaahan karta **hu**n	आह्वाहन करता **था** - I called Ahwaahan karta **tha**

Preterite And Perfect	Pluperfect
आह्वाहन किया **हुआ** - It is called Ahwaahan kiya **hua**	आह्वाहन किया **था** - I had called Ahwaahan kiya **tha**

Future And Immediate Future	Immediate Past Future
आह्वाहन करूँगा - I will call Ahwaahan karun**ga**	आह्वाहन करने वाला **था** - I was about to call Ahwaahan karne vala **tha**

Imperative

Single And Polite	Future Polite
आह्वाहन **करिए** - Do call Ahwaahan **kariye**	आह्वाहन कीजिए**गा** - Please call Ahwaahan kijie**gaa**

Subjunctive

Present	Habitual And Continuous
आह्वाहन **करूँ** – Do I call Ahwaahan **karoon**	आह्वाहन करता **हूँ** – I call Ahwaahan karta **hu**n

Perfect And Immediate Future
आह्वाहन करा **हूँ** - I have called Ahwaahan kara **hu**n

Conditional

Present And Habitual	Continuous And Preterite
आह्वाहन **करता** - He calls Ahwaahan karta	आह्वाहन कर रहा **होता** - He would be calling Ahwaahan **kar** raha **hota**

Presumptive

Present And Imperfective	Continuous And Future Perfect
आह्वाहन करता **हूँगा** – I would be calling. Ahwaahan karta **hunga**	आह्वाहन कर रहा **हूँगा** - I would have been calling. Ahwaahan **kar** raha **hunga**

Infinitive	Can	सक्षम होना Saksham hona

Indicative

Present	Past
सक्षम **हूँ** - I can Saksham **hu**n	सक्षम **था** - I could Saksham **tha**

Preterite And Perfect	Pluperfect
सक्षम **हुआ** – It could Saksham **hua**	सक्षम **हुआ था** - I could Saksham **hua tha**

Future And Immediate Future	Immediate Past Future
सक्षम होऊँगा - I could Saksham **hunga**a	सक्षम होने वाला **था** - I could have Saksham hone vala **tha**

Imperative

Single And Polite	Future Polite
सक्षम होइए - Can Saksham hoiye	सक्षम होईएगा - Please you could Saksham hoiegaa

Subjunctive

Present	Habitual And Continuous
सक्षम होऊँ - I can Saksham houn	सक्षम **होता हूँ** - I can Saksham **hota hu**n

Perfect And Immediate Future
सक्षम **होता** - I could have Saksham **hu**n

Conditional	

Present And Habitual	Continuous And Preterite
सक्षम **होता** - He can Saksham **hota**	सक्षम हो रहा **होता** - He would be Saksham ho raha **hota**

Presumptive	

Present And Imperfective	Continuous And Future Perfect
सक्षम **होता हूँगा** – I would be Saksham **hota hunga**	सक्षम हो रहा **हूँगा**- I would have been Saksham ho raha **hunga**

Infinitive	To Choose	चुनाव करना Chunav karna

Indicative

Present	Past
चुनाव करता हूँ - I choose Chunav karta **hu**n	चुनाव करता **था** - I chose Chunav karta **tha**

Preterite And Perfect	Pluperfect
चुनाव किया **हुआ** - It is chosen Chunav kiya **hua**	चुनाव किया **था** - I had chosen Chunav kiya **tha**

Future And Immediate Future	Immediate Past Future
चुनाव करूँगा - I will choose Chunav karun**ga**	चुनाव करने वाला **था** - I was about to choose Chunav karne vala **tha**

Imperative	

Single And Polite	Future Polite
चुनाव **करिए** - Do choose Chunav **kariye**	चुनाव कीजिए**गा** - Please choose Chunav kijie**ga**

Subjunctive	

Present	Habitual And Continuous
चुनाव **करूँ** - Do I choose Chunav **karoo**	चुनाव करता **हूँ** - I choose Chunav karta **hu**n

Perfect And Immediate Future
चुनाव किया है - I have chosen Chunav kiya hai

Conditional

Present And Habitual	Continuous And Preterite
चुनाव **करता** - He chooses Chunav karta	चुनाव कर रहा **होता** - He would be choosing Chunav **kar** raha **hota**

Presumptive

Present And Imperfective	Continuous And Future Perfect
चुनाव करता **हूँगा** – I would be choosing. Chunav karta **hunga**	चुनाव कर रहा **हूँगा**- I would have been choosing. Chunav **kar** raha **hunga**

Infinitive	To Close	बंद करना Band karna

Indicative

Present	Past
बंद करता हूँ - I close Band karta **hun**	बंद करता **था** - I closed Band karta **tha**

Preterite And Perfect	Pluperfect
बंद किया **हुआ** - It is closed Band kiya **hua**	बंद किया **था** - I had closed Band kiya **tha**

Future And Immediate Future	Immediate Past Future
बंद करूँगा - I will close Band karun**ga**a	बंद करने वाला **था** - I was about to close Band karne vala **tha**

Imperative

Single And Polite	Future Polite
बंद **करिए** - Do close Band **kariye**	बंद कीजिए**गा** - Please close Band kijie**ga**

Subjunctive

Present	Habitual And Continuous
बंद **करूँ** - Do I close Band **karun**	बंद करता **हूँ** - I close Band karta **hun**

Perfect And Immediate Future
बंद करा **हूँ** - I have closed Band kara **hu**n

Conditional

Present And Habitual	Continuous And Preterite
बंद **करता** - He closes Band karta	बंद कर रहा **होता** - He would be closing Band **kar** raha **hota**

Presumptive

Present And Imperfective	Continuous And Future Perfect
बंद करता **हूँगा** – I would be closing. Band karta **hunga**	बंद कर रहा **हूँगा**- I would have been closing. Band **kar** raha **hunga**

Infinitive	To Come	आना Aana

Indicative

Present	Past
आता हूँ - I come Aata **hun**	आता **था** - I came Aata **tha**

Preterite And Perfect	Pluperfect
आया **हुआ** - It came Aaya **hua**	आया **था** - I had come Aaya **tha**

Future And Immediate Future	Immediate Past Future
आऊंगा - I will come Aaun**ga**	आने वाला **था** - I was about to come Aane vala **tha**

Imperative	

Single And Polite	Future Polite
आया **करिए** - Do come Aaya **kariye**	आया करिएगा - Please come Aaya kariyega

Subjunctive	

Present	Habitual And Continuous
आया **करूँ** - Do I come Aaya **karoon**	आता हूँ - I come Aata **hu**n

Perfect And Immediate Future
आया हूँ - I have come Aaya **hu**n

Conditional

Present And Habitual	Continuous And Preterite
आता - He comes Aata	आ रहा **होता** - He would be coming Aa raha **hota**

Presumptive

Present And Imperfective	Continuous And Future Perfect
आता **हूँगा** – I would be coming. Aata ra**hunga**	आ रहा **हूँगा**- I would have been coming. Aar aha **hunga**

Infinitive	To Cook	भोजन बनाना Bhojan banana

Indicative

Present	Past
भोजन बनाता हूँ - I cook Bhojan banata **hun**	भोजन बनाता **था** - I cooked Bhojan banata **tha**

Preterite And Perfect	Pluperfect
भोजन बनाया **हुआ** - It is cooked Bhojan banaya **hua**	भोजन बनाया **था** - I had cooked Bhojan banaya **tha**

Future And Immediate Future	Immediate Past Future
भोजन बनाउन्गा- I will cook Bhojan banun**ga**a	भोजन बनाने वाला **था** - I was about to cook Bhojan banane vala **tha**

Imperative

Single And Polite	Future Polite
भोजन बनाईए - Do cook Bhojan banaiye	भोजन बनाएगा - Please cook Bhojan banaegaa

Subjunctive

Present	Habitual And Continuous
भोजन बनाऊं- Do I cook Bhojan banau	भोजन बनाता हूँ - I cook Bhojan banata hun

Perfect And Immediate Future
भोजन बनाया हूँ - I have cooked Bhojan banaya hua

Conditional

Present And Habitual	Continuous And Preterite
भोजन बनाता - He cooks Bhojan banata	भोजन बना रहा **होता** - He would be cooking Bhojan bana raha **hota**

Presumptive

Present And Imperfective	Continuous And Future Perfect
भोजन बनाता **हूँगा** – I would be cooking. Bhojan banata **hunga**	भोजन बना रहा **हूँगा**- I would have been cooking. Bhojan bana raha **hunga**

Infinitive	To Cry	रुदन करना Rudan karna

Indicative

Present	Past
रुदन करता हूँ - I cry Rudan karta **hun**	रुदन करता **था** - I cried Rudan karta **tha**

Preterite And Perfect	Pluperfect
रुदन किया **हुआ** - It is cried Rudan kiya **hua**	रुदन किया **था** - I had cried Rudan kiya **tha**

Future And Immediate Future	Immediate Past Future
रुदन करूँगा - I will cry Rudan karun**ga**	रुदन करने वाला **था** - I was about to cry Rudan karne vala **tha**

Imperative

Single And Polite	Future Polite
रुदन **करिए** - Do cry Rudan **kariye**	रुदन कीजिए**गा** - Please cry Rudan kijie**ga**

Subjunctive

Present	Habitual And Continuous
रुदन **करूँ** – Do I cry Rudan **karun**	रुदन करता **हूँ** - I cry Rudan karta **hun**

Perfect And Immediate Future
रुदन करा **हूँ** - I have cried Rudan kara **hu**n

Conditional

Present And Habitual	Continuous And Preterite
रुदन **करता** - He cries Rudan karta	रुदन कर रहा **होता** - He would be crying Rudan **kar** raha **hota**

Presumptive

Present And Imperfective	Continuous And Future Perfect
रुदन करता **हूँगा** – I would be crying. Rudan karta **hunga**	रुदन कर रहा **हूँगा**- I would have been crying. Rudan **kar** raha **hunga**